D1258349

Official Financing for Developing Countries

Prepared by a Staff Team in the Policy Development
and Review Department led by Michael G. Kuhn

Przemyslaw Gajdeczka
Christopher J. Jarvis
Toshiyuki Kosugi
Keon Hyok Lee
Pichit Patrawimolpon

INTERNATIONAL MONETARY FUND
Washington, DC
April 1994

ISBN 1-55775-378-4
ISSN 0258-7440

Price: US$20.00
(US$12.00 to full-time faculty members and
students at universities and colleges)

Please send orders to:
International Monetary Fund, Publication Services
700 19th Street, N.W., Washington, D.C. 20431, U.S.A.
Tel.: (202) 623-7430   Telefax: (202) 623-7201

recycled paper

Contents

Page

Preface

This paper was prepared in the Policy Development and Review Department of the International Monetary Fund, under the direction of Michael G. Kuhn, Chief of the Official Financing Operations Division. Its authors are Przemyslaw Gajdeczka, Christopher J. Jarvis, Toshiyuki Kosugi, Keon Hyok Lee, and Pichit Patrawimolpon, economists in the division. Helpful contributions were also made by Anthony Boote and Matthew Fisher. The paper provides information on official financing for developing countries with a particular focus on the low- and lower middle-income rescheduling countries. It updates information contained in *Official Multilateral Debt Rescheduling: Recent Experience*, World Economic and Financial Surveys (Washington: IMF, November 1990) and also reviews recent developments in direct financing by official and multilateral sources.

The work benefited from comments by staff in other departments of the IMF and by members of the Executive Board. Opinions expressed, however, are those of the authors and do not necessarily represent the views of the IMF or its Executive Directors. The study was completed in November 1993 and reflects developments to that time.

The authors are grateful to Hassanin A. Ismeail for research, and Ann-Barbara Hyde for secretarial assistance, and are particularly indebted to Sulochana Kamaldinni for coordinating the processing of the document. Juanita Roushdy of the External Relations Department edited the manuscript and coordinated production.

I

Overview

Three broad trends characterize recent developments in financing flows to developing countries. First, official financing flows have continued to increase at a rapid pace with *net* flows rising to $72 billion in 1992 from some $44 billion in 1985. Second, the form and terms of official financial assistance have become differentiated, reflecting the diverse situations and prospects facing different groups of developing countries. Particularly noteworthy is the continuing shift by both multilateral and bilateral creditors toward highly concessional financing for the low-income countries. Third, official creditors and donors have increasingly linked the availability of new financing to countries' policy environments and performance under adjustment programs. The buildup in official support has been most pronounced for countries that established a record of policy performance; for those countries with mixed records of policy implementation, resources were less readily available. Overall, reflecting these trends, by far the most important source of financing for the vast majority of developing countries over the past decade has been official bilateral and multilateral creditors.

The paper focuses mainly on official bilateral and multilateral financing for countries that have rescheduled their debts to official bilateral creditors. In contrast to the approaches taken by private lenders, official creditors have continued to provide new financing on a large scale to countries with debt-servicing difficulties that implement adjustment and reform programs. Financial support has been provided through a wide variety of instruments and channels. Direct support from official bilateral sources has taken the form of financing through grants and loans, often on concessional terms. Indirect support has been given through insurance and guarantees by official export credit agencies for credits extended by the private sector, as well as through comprehensive cash-flow relief on official bilateral debt through the Paris Club. Multilateral financial institutions, including the International Monetary Fund (IMF), have provided a substantial and increasing share of financing, including support for debt-reduction operations on commercial bank debt.

Recent years have seen a rapid change in the debt situations of the rescheduling countries, and their experiences have been markedly different. Most of the major middle-income rescheduling countries have made significant progress in resolving their debt problems, in the context of comprehensive macroeconomic adjustment and structural reform programs, and some have regained access to spontaneous private financing. Many other middle-income rescheduling countries are well advanced in re-establishing normal relations with creditors. The debt situation of the low-income and some of the lower middle-income rescheduling countries, however, remains very difficult.

Section II takes stock of recent external debt developments in these countries. While they share a number of common characteristics, the country-specific review reveals a wide variety of circumstances. The most striking feature is that heavy scheduled debt-service burdens have not resulted in net resource transfers to creditors. Instead, most of the rescheduling countries continued to obtain large, and in many cases increasing, net inflows of resources. Official creditors recognized these countries' protracted balance of payments difficulties and heavy reliance on external financing for essential import and development needs. Their strategy aimed primarily at ensuring the availability of adequate financing in support of countries' adjustment programs, and crucial to the success of this strategy has been the maintenance of cutoff dates in successive reschedulings. It enabled official bilateral creditors to provide assistance in the form of new financial flows while at the same time granting cash-flow relief on existing "pre-cutoff date" official bilateral debt.

For the low-income rescheduling countries as a group, total financial assistance has been about as large as these countries' own export earnings in every year since 1986. Heavy indebtedness has thus not been associated with heavy actual debt-service burdens, which remained relatively low for most rescheduling countries. While countries that sustained their adjustment efforts and maintained broadly satisfactory relations with creditors typically made significant debt payments, they found that the payments were more than offset by inflows of new direct financial assistance. In contrast, countries with mixed records of performance, including the accumulation of external arrears for prolonged periods, saw their access to new financing reduced.

Creditors have implemented a wide range of measures to alleviate debt burdens in recent years. The measures included greater concessionality in new lending for the low-income countries, major bilateral debt forgiveness initiatives, and reschedulings for low-income countries on increasingly concessional terms. As a result of the shift toward greater concessionality in new lending by both official bilateral and multilateral creditors, debt-service payments on post-cutoff date official bilateral debt and on multilateral debt are relatively small for all but a very few countries. The measures on pre-cutoff date debt—concessionality in reschedulings and bilateral debt forgiveness—helped slow the pace of deterioration but were not sufficient to bring about a decisive improvement in the debt-service profile in most of the low-income rescheduling cases. Debt-service profiles remain dominated by debt obligations resulting from earlier reschedulings on nonconcessional terms. This is particularly true for those countries where initially high debts and small shares of concessional debt meant greater reliance on debt reschedulings as a source of financing, and where debt-service obligations on rescheduled debt grew at a faster rate than countries' capacity to make payments on such debts.

Paris Club creditors have become more aware that a durable solution to the debt problem of the low-income countries calls for a fundamental reorganization of the stock of pre-cutoff date debt. In December 1991, they adopted a phased approach to debt restructuring, which combined continued flow reschedulings on more concessional terms with consideration of a debt-stock operation after a track record of adjustment had been established. Section II, inter alia, examines the impact on countries' debt-service profiles of such possible debt-stock operations by Paris Club and other bilateral and private creditors. A number of broad conclusions emerge.

First, while the terms of the stock operations are yet to be determined, the approach followed by the Paris Club, if implemented with sufficient flexibility, should be adequate to deal decisively with the debt problems of most of the low-income rescheduling countries. A debt-reduction incorporating a 50 percent reduction in net present value terms would go a long way to reduce the debt-service profile on restructurable debt to managable levels. Substantially deeper reductions, however, will be required in a number of cases to reduce debt-service payments to levels that can be sustained, even in the context of ambitious and sustained adjustment programs.

Second, the solution to the debt problem of some rescheduling countries lies largely outside the Paris Club. Some of these countries require special action

by non-Paris Club creditors. These creditors have already shown considerable flexibility.

Third, a few countries are heavily indebted to multilateral institutions. They are therefore particularly dependent on adequate new flows on concessional terms in support of continued policy adjustment.

Fourth, given their long-term development needs, these countries will continue to require large amounts of external financing. It is crucial that debt-restructuring operations do not reduce new financial flows. To be sustainable, the profile of restructured debt must feature flat or only gradually rising payments, and the rate of increase must be well below the projected rate of export growth. This will make room for debt service on nonrestructurable debts and new financial flows. The magnitude of resource requirements also means that the role for debt-creating flows is very limited. Instead, these countries will have to rely on grants and highly concessional loans for most of their financing needs and on increasing direct investment.

Finally, debtor countries must strengthen and broaden their adjustment and reform efforts. While external debt problems have contributed to their protracted balance of payments difficulties, heavy indebtedness has not been a fundamental obstacle to growth and development in the low-income rescheduling countries. Conversely, the resolution of external debt problems by itself cannot be expected to lead to a fundamental improvement in the economic and financial situation and prospects unless accompanied by comprehensive and sustained macroeconomic adjustment and structural reform. As the experience of recent graduates from the rescheduling process demonstrates, a return to normal debtor-creditor relationships is a necessary, but far from sufficient, condition for these countries to attract non-debt-creating flows, which are essential for long-term development and growth, and, in particular direct foreign investment.

Against this background, the subsequent sections of the paper provide more detailed information on recent developments in the three main areas of official financial support: debt reschedulings, direct financial flows from official bilateral sources, and lending by multilateral institutions. Section III reviews recent developments in official bilateral debt restructurings from three perspectives. Its main focus is on recent experience with debt reschedulings in the multilateral framework of the Paris Club. It also reviews recent debt renegotiations involving official bilateral creditors that are not participating in the Paris Club, and reports on recent debt forgiveness initiatives that have been implemented on a bilateral basis.

Section IV reports on recent developments in

direct financing from official bilateral creditors, with particular emphasis on the various instruments of support, and on experience in financing of the rescheduling countries. It brings out clearly the three main features of recent experience: increases in the overall levels of financial support, increasing adaptation of the terms to country circumstances, and increasing links to the implementation of appropriate adjustment policies.

Section V provides information on lending by multilateral institutions, including the IMF. The review highlights three major developments that mirror the three broad trends characterizing official bilateral financing in recent years. First, multilateral lending has increased sharply both in absolute terms and as a share of total financing flows to developing countries. Second, countries that established a strong record of sustained policy implementation witnessed the most pronounced increase in multilateral lending. Third, multilateral institutions have increasingly adapted the terms of their

lending to country circumstances and this has been reflected in a marked shift toward concessional lending to the low-income countries. As a consequence, debt-service obligations to multilateral creditors have increased only modestly and at a much slower rate than the stock of debt owed to these creditors. In a few cases, however, where the shift toward concessional financing has been less pronounced, in part because of mixed adjustment records, obligations to multilateral institutions remain substantial.

These recent trends in official financing have important ramifications for developing countries. Access to external financing from official sources is likely to remain high for those countries whose adjustment and reform efforts provide assurances that resources will be used efficiently. Conversely, countries with uneven records of policy implementation (particularly as regards payments arrears) are likely to find difficulty in attracting financial support.

II

The External Debt of Rescheduling Countries

This section reviews external debt developments of countries that have rescheduled their official bilateral debts in the framework of the Paris Club since 1980. The middle-income countries, which are mainly indebted to commercial creditors, have made substantial progress in resolving their debt problems. An increasing number of debtors have reached agreements with their commercial bank creditors on debt-restructuring packages, and some have regained access to spontaneous financing.

Debt problems remain serious, however, for most of the low- and lower middle-income rescheduling countries mainly indebted to official creditors. Official creditors have continued to provide financial support, often on a large scale, to countries implementing appropriate adjustment policies. This strategy has proven successful in a number of the lower middle-income countries that are making good progress in graduating from the rescheduling process. For the vast majority of low-income countries, and a few of the lower middle-income countries, however, a durable solution to their debt problems has remained elusive.

Official creditors have implemented a wide range of measures to alleviate debt burdens and provided large-scale new financial assistance on increasingly concessional terms. These measures helped but were not sufficient to bring about a decisive improvement in the debt situation. The prospects for continued dependence on future reschedulings with uncertain terms and coverage, and uncertainties regarding the magnitude and timing of prospective disbursements of direct financial assistance, complicated economic and financial management. This contributed to difficulties in sustaining adjustment programs, especially during periods of terms of trade declines. An accumulation of external arrears usually accompanied breaks in the adjustment process and further exacerbated already difficult situations. Even with sustained adjustment efforts, most of these countries would require cash-flow relief for many years to come. As Paris Club creditors have recognized, more definitive action on the stock of restructurable debt is needed to provide the low-income rescheduling countries with the clear prospect of an exit from the rescheduling process.

The Setting

Since 1980, 58 countries have needed to reschedule their official bilateral debt (Table 1). Paris Club reschedulings have generally paralleled the sharp rise in commercial bank debt restructurings but were less concentrated around the onset of the generalized debt crisis in the early 1980s. This reflected the more diversified experience of countries largely indebted to official creditors, in part because these creditors did not abruptly change their lending practices. Fifteen countries had approached the Paris Club already during 1976–82, before the emergence of more widespread debt-servicing difficulties. During the following three years, 1983–85, 19 others obtained Paris Club reschedulings, mostly middle-income countries with large debts to private creditors. Since 1986 another 24 countries have required reschedulings in the Paris Club.

Most of the rescheduling countries have returned to the Paris Club time after time; 19 have obtained five or more reschedulings. The longest cumulative period covered by consolidations extends for more than thirteen years, and for nearly one half of the rescheduling countries the cumulative consolidation period exceeds five years. In most cases, the period of effective cash-flow relief was considerably longer because successive consolidations were seldom negotiated in an unbroken sequence (Chart 1).

Progress in resolving debt difficulties through successive reschedulings remained slow. To date, only 14 of the 58 countries have resumed normal relations with creditors. Successful graduates from the Paris Club rescheduling process were mostly those middle-income countries that had been predominantly indebted to private creditors. Their success was based on the sustained implementation of macroeconomic and structural reform policies, often accompanied by comprehensive commercial bank debt restructurings.[1] For the other middle-

---

[1]Recent developments in commercial bank debt restructurings are reported in *Private Market Financing for Developing Countries*, World Economic and Financial Surveys (Washington: International Monetary Fund, December 1993).

Table 1. Debt-Rescheduling Countries

(As of the end of September 1993)

| | Agreements | | Cumulative | | | Agreements | | Cumulative | |
	First	Number	Period	Status[1]		First	Number	Period	Status[1]
Low-income countries			*(In months)*		**Middle-income countries**			*(In months)*	
Angola	1989	1	15	Arrears	Argentina	1985	5	83	Current
Benin	1989	3	61	Current	Brazil	1983	4	87	Graduated
Bolivia	1986	4	69	Current	Bulgaria	1991	2	17	Arrears
Burkina Faso	1991	2	48	Current	Cameroon	1989	2	21	Arrears
Central African					Chile	1985	2	39	Graduated
Republic	1981	5	72	Arrears					
Chad	1989	1	15	Arrears	Congo	1986	2	41	Arrears
Equatorial Guinea	1985	3	30	Arrears	Costa Rica	1983	5	56	Graduated
Ethiopia	1992	1	35	Current	Côte d'Ivoire	1984	6	81	Arrears
Gambia, The	1986	1	12	Graduated	Dominican Republic	1985	2	33	Graduated
Guinea	1986	3	26	Arrears	Ecuador	1983	5	64	Arrears
Guinea-Bissau	1987	2	33	Arrears	Egypt	1987	2	55	Current
Guyana	1989	3	66	Current	El Salvador	1990	1	13	Graduated
Honduras	1990	2	52	Current	Gabon	1978	5	58	Arrears
Liberia	1980	4	60	Arrears	Guatemala	1993	1	—	Graduated
Madagascar	1981	7	121	Arrears	Jamaica	1984	7	127	Current
Malawi	1982	3	38	Graduated	Jordan	1989	2	36	Current
Mali	1988	3	77	Current	Mexico	1983	3	60	Graduated
Mauritania	1985	5	77	Current	Morocco	1983	6	86	Graduated
Mozambique	1984	4	85	Current	Nigeria	1986	3	46	Arrears
Nicaragua	1991	1	15	Arrears	Panama	1985	2	33	Graduated
Niger	1983	7	103	Arrears	Peru	1978	5	93	Current
Senegal	1981	9	120	Arrears	Philippines	1984	4	75	. . .[2]
Sierra Leone	1977	5	84	Current	Poland	1981	6	119	Current
Somalia	1985	2	36	Arrears	Romania	1982	2	24	Graduated
Sudan	1979	4	63	Arrears	Russian Federation	1993	1	12	Current
Tanzania	1986	4	60	Current	Trinidad and Tobago	1989	2	27	Graduated
Togo	1979	9	162	Arrears	Turkey	1978	3	61	Graduated
Uganda	1981	5	71	Current	Yugoslavia, former				
Zambia	1983	5	87	Current	Socialist Federal				
Zaïre	1976	10	131	Arrears	Republic of	1984	4	67	. . .

Sources: Debt-rescheduling agreements; and IMF staff estimates.

[1]Current = rescheduling agreement effective; arrears = accumulating arrears on debt to Paris Club creditors; graduated = resumed full debt-servicing to Paris Club creditors.

[2]Consolidation period expired, no arrears, but expect to return to Paris Club.

income countries that currently continue to require cash-flow relief from Paris Club creditors, prospects are generally favorable. Most are expected to graduate over the next few years, although a number in the lower middle-income range continue to face very difficult situations.

In contrast to this broadly favorable recent experience of the middle-income countries, the debt situation of the low-income rescheduling countries (most of which are in sub-Saharan Africa) has remained intractable. These countries continue to rely heavily on debt reschedulings despite large-scale direct assistance by official creditors in the form of new loans and grants (see Sections IV and V), actions by private creditors to reduce debt, official bilateral debt forgiveness initiatives, and recent moves toward concessions in reschedulings.

This protracted reliance on debt reschedulings by most low-income and some of the lower middle-income rescheduling countries can be traced to two interdependent factors. First, most have experienced long-lasting and, in many cases, very sharp declines in their terms of trade, and have thus faced severe structural and balance of payments difficulties. Had the severity and persistence of the external shocks been fully anticipated at the outset, stronger adjustment efforts and financing on more appropriate terms would have been called for. While many of these countries embarked on adjustment programs supported by the IMF, other multilateral institutions, and official bilateral creditors, many experienced difficulty in sustaining their adjustment efforts. This reflected in part the severity and duration of the terms of trade shock. Breaks

Chart 1: Renegotiations of Official Bilateral Debt, Consolidation Periods of Successive Rescheduling Agreements, 1982–June 1993

Country	1982	1983	1984	1985	1986	1987	1988	1989	1990	1991	1992	1993	1994	1995	1996	Country
Zaïre	-----------	< 6----------	7-----------	---8-------	--<9---------	------		<10---	-------		<5-	---*--------	--			Zaïre
Sierra Leone		< 3-----------		<4-------	------------											Sierra Leone
Gabon				2---	------------	3----------		<4- ------------	<5--	------------						Gabon
Peru		2-------	----3-------	-------					<4--	------------	5-----------	---*--------	---*--------	--		Peru
Togo	----------<	3-----------	4-------	-----5-------	----	<	6-----------	----7-------	-------8-----	---------*--	------9-----	-----*-----	------			Togo
Sudan	-----------<	3-----------	4------------													Sudan
Liberia	2--------*--	------3-----	------4-----	------												Liberia
Poland	2-----------	------------	------------	3----------		<	4-----------	<	5-----------	-------6-------		---**				Poland
Madagascar	----<2-----	---<3----	4----------	---5-----	-----------*	--<6-------	-----*------	----7-----	------							Madagascar
Central African Republic	< 2-----------		3-----	------------			<	4----*------<5----------								Central African Republic
Senegal	-----2-----	------3-----	------	<	4-----------	------5-----	-------6-----	---------7-	------------	<8---------	<9----	------				Senegal
Uganda	------2-----	------					<3----	------	<	4----*-----	------------	<5---*				Uganda
Costa Rica	<1----	------------		<	2-----------	---			<3----	------	<4----	---	<5			Costa Rica
Zambia		<	1-----------<2-----------			<3-----------				< 4----	*-----------	<5----	----*-----	----*-------	---	Zambia
Mexico		<1-----				2---	------------	---		3-----	---*---------	---*--------	------			Mexico
Ecuador		1-------	-----	<	2-----------	------------	------------<	3----------	--	<4	------------	<5----------				Ecuador
Morocco		<1---	------------		<2--	------------	---3--------	----4-------	------------	<5--	---	6----------				Morocco
Niger		1--	-------2--	----------3	------4	------5	------------	6---------		<7---	---	*--	----------			Niger
Brazil		<1---	------------	2-----------	------------	*-----		<3---	------	---	<4-----	---*------				Brazil
Côte d'Ivoire		1	-----------	2-----------	3-----------		<	4-----------	<	5----------*-	-----	<6--	----------			Côte d'Ivoire
Jamaica		<	1-----------	---2-----	---	<	3-----------	----*-4-----	----------5	------------	---6-------	------	7--	------*-----	------*-------	Jamaica
Mozambique		<1-----	------		<2-----	------	<3----	---*-------	---------*-	------------	4-----------	------*------				Mozambique
Philippines			1----------	------		2-----------	-------*--	<3----	---*-------	------------4	-------*---	*--				Philippines
Argentina		<	1----------			<2-----	------------	<	3----------	---	<4--	------5-----	------*-----	------*-----	---	Argentina
Somalia		<	1-----------	<	2-----------	------------										Somalia
Mauritania		<	1-----------	---2-----	---3--------	------		<4-----	------------		<	5----------	*-----------			Mauritania
Dominican Republic		<	1-----------	------						<2--	------------	---				Dominican Republic
Equatorial Guinea		<	1-----------	------		<	2			<3----------					Equatorial Guinea
Panama			<1---	------------					<2	------------	---				Panama
Guinea			1-----------	--		<	2-----------			<	3				Guinea
Bolivia					<1----	------	<2---	--------*---	3----------	*-----------	4-----*------	------				Bolivia
Congo					<1--	------------	---		<2---	------------						Congo
Tanzania					<1--	---------	<	2-----	< 3-----------		<4----*-----	------*-----	------			Tanzania
Nigeria					<1---	------------	------	<	2-----------	----	<3----------	---				Nigeria
Egypt					<	1-----------	------------				2----------	-----*-------	-----*------	---**		Egypt
Guinea-Bissau						<1-----	------	<2---	------*-----		<3--	------*----	------*---	-------		Guinea-Bissau
Mali							<1-----	---------<2	-----*------	*----------						Mali
Guyana							<	1----------	--	<2---	------*-----	------*-----	-------3----	------------		Guyana
Cameroon							<1-----	---			<2-------					Cameroon
Benin							<1-----	------		<	2---------	-------3----	*----------	*-----------		Benin
Jordan							<1-----	------------		<2-----	------------*-----	--				Jordan
Angola							<1-----	---------								Angola
Chad							<1-	------------								Chad
Honduras								<1---	------	------*-----	--	<2--	------*----	------*----	------	Honduras
Burkina Faso									<1--------	-----		<2-------	*----------	*-----------		Burkina Faso
Bulgaria										<1-------	---	<2 ----				Bulgaria
Nicaragua										<	1-----------	---				Nicaragua
Ethiopia											<1	-----*-	---------*-	----------		Ethiopia
Russian Federation											<	1----------				Russian Federation
Guatemala												<1				Guatemala

Sources: Agreed Minutes of debt reschedulings; and Fund staff estimates.

Notes: 1, 2, 3, etc. - Indicates the start of succsessive consolidation periods since 1976 (see Appendix I, Table 1).

    * - Indicates conditional future rescheduling or extension of consolidation period.

    ** - Indicates agreement to restructure stock value of debt.

    < - Indicates consolidation date of arrears.

[1] The following countries that have graduated from official multilateral debt rescheduling through end-1991are no longer included in the chart: Chile, El Salvador, The Gambia, Malawi, Romania, Yugoslavia, Trinidad & Tobago, and Turkey. Representation of dates is approximate.

Box 1. Measures of the Debt Burden

Measuring the debt burden in the low- and lower middle-income countries presents a number of problems. The conventional index, the stock of debt relative to the resource base, such as exports of goods and services, can be seriously misleading.[1] This index fails to capture the effects of new financing and of debt relief on more concessional terms, that is, lower interest rates and longer repayment periods. An attractive conceptual alternative would be to compare the present value of future debt-service obligations with the present value of future export receipts. This approach suffers, however, from a number of serious drawbacks: the sensitivity to the discount rate assumed, the uncertainty about future export receipts, and the exceptionally complex data requirements.[2] Moreover, even if these difficulties could be overcome, the computed ratio would provide little or no information about the debt-service profile. It would not be operationally relevant to the most pressing concerns of the rescheduling countries under review: the immediate cash-flow requirement of debt-service obligations and the need to establish a managable medium-term debt-service profile.

In this paper, the debt burden is viewed mainly in terms of three debt-service ratios: the ratio of the scheduled total debt-service payments (i.e., principal plus interest) to exports, the ratio of scheduled interest payments to exports, and the ratio of actual debt-service payments to exports. These ratios are more readily available and capture changes in concessionality. The three ratios measure different aspects of the debt burden: **the ratio of debt service to exports** reflects the potential impact of debt-service obligations on foreign exchange cash flow, **the scheduled interest-to-exports ratio** measures the ongoing cost of the accumulated stock of debt, and **the ratio of actual debt service to exports** indicates the impact of actual debt service paid on the foreign exchange cash flow.

The first two ratios tell generally the same story, largely because they are influenced in the same way by developments in exports. Moreover, increases in the concessionality of interest rates are typically reinforced by lengthened repayment periods on new lending by both bilateral and multilateral sources. In the present context, however, debt-service profiles are typically dominated by the effects of reschedulings. For many countries under review, grace periods from earlier reschedulings on shorter maturities have expired and amortization payments arising from these reschedulings account for a large part of total scheduled debt-service payments. Thus, in many cases where the scheduled interest ratio declined because of increased concessionality in new lending and in reschedulings, the total scheduled debt-service ratio remained broadly unchanged.

The gap between the actual and scheduled debt-service ratio measures the extent to which countries were unable to make debt-service payments on schedule and relied on debt-related exceptional financing—defined here as the sum of rescheduling from all sources and the net accumulation of external debt arrears. Actual debt-service ratios have been lowest for countries during periods of arrears accumulation, the most disorderly form of external financing. Actual debt-service ratios are typically higher once rescheduling agreements are reached, debt-service payments are resumed and the regularization of relations with creditors leads to inflows of new financing. Finally, countries with the highest actual debt-service ratios tend to be those that are committed to a resumption of or maintenance of normal relations with creditors.

---

[1]In this paper, debt and debt service are viewed relative to exports rather than GDP because export data are more accurate and comprehensive than GDP data and because changes in real exchange rates, which were large during recent years, produce sharp changes in ratios of debt to GDP.

[2]The World Bank has used a variant of this measure—the ratio of the present value of future debt-service payments to current exports.

---

in the adjustment process were usually accompanied by an accumulation of external arrears. This undermined countries' efforts to re-establish creditworthiness and reduced their access to new financing from official sources, including, in particular, loans on concessional terms. In these circumstances, many countries had to rely on repeated and increasingly comprehensive reschedulings and, in some cases, an accumulation of arrears, which further exacerbated already difficult situations.

Second, the move toward greater concessionality in new lending and toward grant financing gathered pace only in the late 1980s. Moreover, Paris Club reschedulings were based on market-related interest rates for the low-income countries until late 1988 and provided initially for short repayment periods. As countries found themselves unable to meet the obligations arising from previous reschedulings, they required increasingly comprehensive cash-flow relief. This, in turn, resulted in obligations on rescheduled debts rising at a faster rate than the country's capacity to service such debts.

In the following sections, the review focuses on a variety of measures of the debt burden (Box 1) and the classification for the countries is based on the terms they obtained most recently in Paris Club

Table 2. Lower Middle-Income Rescheduling Countries: Debt and Debt-Export Ratios by Country, 1986–92

	External Debt 1992	Debt-to-Exports Ratio[1] 1986	Debt-to-Exports Ratio[1] 1992	Changes from 1986 to 1992[2] Debt-to-exports ratio	Changes from 1986 to 1992[2] External debt	Exports Value	Exports Volume	Exports Prices
	(In billions of U.S. dollars)							
Group 1: Improving situation								
Costa Rica	3.4	258	123	−74	−12	63	53	10
Dominican Republic	4.6	263	213	−21	21	41	−44	85
Ecuador	12.4	344	346	—	31	31	20	11
Egypt	35.9	555	332	−51	−6	45	−1	46
Jamaica	4.8	233	192	−19	35	54	40	14
Morocco	17.6	564	263	−76	1	78	30	48
Philippines	32.0	315	185	−53	16	70	52	18
Poland	48.2	292	296	1	24	23	13	10
Average		353	244	−37	14	50	20	30
Group 2: Deteriorating situation								
Bulgaria	13.0	141	316	81	103	22	−141	163
Cameroon	6.7	129	302	85	69	−16	−4	−12
Congo	4.8	356	378	6	51	45	33	12
Côte d'Ivoire	14.3	258	420	49	40	−9	23	−32
Jordan	8.5	168	251	40	49	12	−48	56
Nigeria	29.8	354	235	−41	15	56	31	25
Peru	23.9	417	525	23	49	26	9	17
Average		260	347	35	54	19	−14	33
Average all		310	292	−3	32	35	4	31

Source: IMF staff estimates.
[1]In percent of exports of goods and services.
[2]Index expressed in log normal terms.

reschedulings (see Table A6). The classification differs from those used by the World Bank and other international organizations.[2]

Lower Middle-Income Rescheduling Countries

Much attention has recently been focused on the situation of the lower middle-income countries with continuing debt-servicing difficulties. Most are heavily indebted to official bilateral creditors but have not benefited from concessional treatment in the Paris Club. Moreover, given the structure of their indebtedness, they have generally not been able to achieve a significant reduction in their over-

[2]The World Bank issues a list of low- and lower middle-income countries on an annual basis. Other international organizations use different per capita income levels in their definitions or update their country composition of income groups less frequently (see Table A8). For example, Bolivia and Senegal are classified by the World Bank as lower middle-income countries but are included here among the low-income countries because they obtained concessional reschedulings. By contrast, Nigeria is classified by the World Bank as a low-income country but is included here in the lower middle-income group, as the most recent Paris Club rescheduling did not incorporate concessional terms and because of the structure of its debt.

all debt burden through debt-reduction operations with commercial banks. Despite these common features, the recent experience of these countries—including the evolution of their debt situations—has been markedly different.

This section examines recent developments in the 15 lower middle-income countries that had effective Paris Club agreements in 1992 or were expected to return to the Paris Club in the near future. Nine of these countries have had repeated reschedulings since the early 1980s (Costa Rica, Côte d'Ivoire, Dominican Republic, Ecuador, Jamaica, Morocco, Peru, the Philippines, and Poland). The other six approached the Paris Club only more recently (Bulgaria, Cameroon, Congo, Egypt, Jordan, and Nigeria). The review covers the period since 1986, when the terms of trade of many of these countries deteriorated and resulted in a sharp fall in export earnings. This external shock was further aggravated by increasingly restricted access to financing from nonofficial sources. It also dealt a sharp blow to those countries already in difficulty and led to the emergence of serious debt-servicing difficulties for others that until then had managed to maintain normal relations with their external creditors.

As private creditors withdrew, official bilateral and multilateral sources stepped up their support,

Table 3. Lower Middle-Income Rescheduling Countries: Debt-Service Indicators by Country, 1986–92[1]

(In percent of exports of goods and services)

	Total Scheduled Debt Service		Actual Debt Service		Scheduled Interest Payment	
	1986	1992	1986	1992	1986	1992
Group 1: Improving situation						
Costa Rica	63	19	34	19	26	8
Dominican Republic	48	24	29	20	14	13
Ecuador	81	65	36	35	29	23
Egypt	73	24	55	24	35	13
Jamaica	77	33	56	29	29	12
Morocco	114	45	59	36	29	19
Philippines	51	26	32	17	24	11
Poland	54	19	21	9	22	14
Average	70	32	40	24	26	14
Group 2: Deteriorating situation						
Bulgaria	15	51	15	7	8	16
Cameroon	16	43	16	8	8	24
Congo	66	57	25	22	23	20
Côte d'Ivoire	39	62	28	23	16	31
Jordan	19	42	19	26	8	18
Nigeria	71	69	26	31	29	17
Peru	78	58	25	9	30	38
Average	43	55	22	18	17	23
Average all	58	42	32	21	22	18
Total (weighted average)	50	40	27	18	20	18

Source: IMF staff estimates.
[1]Including the IMF.

but it was not sufficient to cover the rapid rise in scheduled debt-service payments to all creditors (Table A1). Recourse to external financing in the form of reschedulings and also external arrears nearly doubled between 1986 and 1990 but then declined for two main reasons. First, some countries reached comprehensive debt-stock agreements, which resulted in a reduction in scheduled debt-service payments. Second, some countries regained access to international capital markets, which reduced their need for exceptional financing.

Despite these recent improvements, total exceptional financing for these countries exceeded direct financial assistance in the form of grants and loans throughout the period. For many countries, the pattern became more entrenched over time, and the resulting capitalization of interest contributed to a sharp increase in total debt. Actual debt-service payments declined in nominal terms and as a ratio to exports of goods and services (from 27 percent to 18 percent). Moreover, the shift toward financing from official sources (including exceptional financing) led to a marked increase in the share of official creditors in total debt between 1986 and 1992 from about one half to two thirds; nearly all of this

increase was accounted for by bilateral creditors, whose share in the total increased to over 50 percent.[3]

This aggregate picture masks widely divergent trends among the countries. Some made progress toward the resolution of their debt problems and regained access to private capital; others saw their debt situation deteriorate further.

Countries that Made Progress

Eight of the 15 countries experienced an often marked improvement in their situation (Costa Rica, Dominican Republic, Ecuador, Egypt, Jamaica, Morocco, the Philippines, and Poland). Their average debt-export ratio declined sharply over the past six years from over 350 percent to below 250 percent and the scheduled interest ratio dropped from 26 percent to 14 percent (Tables 2 and 3). Three factors were responsible for this recent progress.

---

[3]The payment of claims on export credit insurance in the context of reschedulings accounts for a large part of the increase in the direct exposure of official bilateral creditors (see Chart 10).

Chart 2. Low-Income Rescheduling Countries: Exports, External Financing, and Scheduled Debt Service, 1986–92[1]

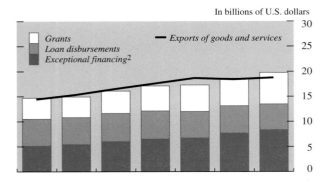

In billions of U.S. dollars

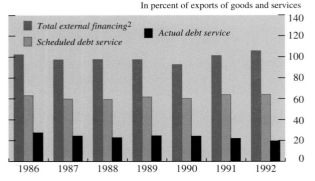

In percent of exports of goods and services

Source: IMF staff estimates.
[1]See Table 1 for listing of countries.
[2]Exceptional financing consists of debt-related financing in the form of debt rescheduling and arrears; total external financing includes exceptional financing.

First, most of the eight countries in the group made sufficient progress in their macroeconomic and structural reforms that the growth of exports significantly exceeded the growth of debt. Export growth was particularly rapid in Costa Rica, Jamaica, Morocco, and the Philippines.

Second, several countries benefited from substantial debt-reduction operations. Costa Rica and the Philippines achieved a sizable reduction of their commercial bank debt; Egypt and Poland obtained an exceptional debt-restructuring from Paris Club creditors; and Egypt and Morocco also benefited from debt forgiveness by non-Paris Club official bilateral creditors. Collectively, these operations helped keep the average growth rate of debt to only 2 percent a year over the period 1986 to 1992.

Third, a number of countries, and in particular Jamaica, Morocco, and the Philippines, managed to maintain broadly satisfactory relations with official bilateral creditors in the context of successive reschedulings. They were thus able to attract large amounts of financial assistance from these creditors

on concessional terms, which helped reduce the average interest rate on outstanding debt to less than 6 percent. While the overall debt situation improved, the debt itself became increasingly concentrated on official creditors.

Some of these lower middle-income countries have already resumed normal relations with creditors (Costa Rica, the Dominican Republic, and Morocco) (Table A2). For most others, an exit from the rescheduling process is a reasonable prospect, provided that they broaden and sustain their adjustment efforts. For countries that obtained debt-stock restructurings from commercial banks (Costa Rica and the Philippines) or official bilateral creditors (Egypt and Poland), scheduled amortization payments have been substantially reduced from 1992 onward. Longer maturities in Paris Club reschedulings for the other countries had a similar but less pronounced effect, and reschedulings might be required in some cases for several more years, given the heavy amortization payments falling due from previous reschedulings. For Ecuador and Poland, further reductions in scheduled debt service could be achieved through commercial bank debt reduction. Such debt operations, combined with continued strong support in the form of new flows, should help bring scheduled payments in line with actual payments capacity and thus eliminate the need for exceptional financing.

Countries Whose Situation Deteriorated

The progress achieved by the first group stands in sharp contrast to the marked deterioration in the debt situations of the other seven countries (Bulgaria, Cameroon, Congo, Côte d'Ivoire, Jordan, Nigeria, and Peru). The cumulative external current account deficits of these countries over the past six years were larger than those of the first group both in relation to exports of goods and services and their initial stock of external debt. These large and growing external imbalances led to a rapid buildup of debt and, as exports grew only marginally, debt and debt-service indicators worsened steadily. For the group as a whole, the ratio of debt to exports of goods and services rose from 260 percent in 1986 to around 350 percent in 1992 (Table 2). Scheduled debt service rose from 43 percent to 55 percent, while actual debt-service payments declined from 22 percent to only 18 percent of exports of goods and services (Table 3). In sharp contrast to the experience of the first group, the scheduled interest ratio rose from 17 percent to 23 percent, reflecting both the rapid buildup of debt and weak export performance. These debt indicators would suggest more difficult prospects for an early return to external viability, even in the context of strong adjustment efforts.

Table 4. Low-Income Rescheduling Countries: Debt and Debt-Export Ratios by Country, 1986–92

| | External Debt | Debt-to-Exports Ratio[1] | | Changes from 1986 to 1992[2] | | | | |
| | | | | Debt-to-exports ratio | External debt | Exports | | |
	1992	1986	1992			Value	Volume	Prices
	(In billions of U.S. dollars)							
Angola	8.0	208	218	5	97	92	67	25
Benin	1.2	182	264	37	52	15	−24	38
Bolivia	5.6	562	720	25	33	8	50	−42
Burkina Faso	1.1	308	283	−9	56	36	14	50
Central African Republic	0.7	215	530	90	61	−29	−42	13
Chad	0.6	56	249	149	199	50	60	−10
Equatorial Guinea	0.2	330	426	26	72	47	58	−11
Ethiopia	4.1	511	734	36	15	−22	−22	—
Gambia, The	0.3	254	125	−71	16	86	40	46
Guinea	2.6	315	354	12	32	20	9	11
Guinea-Bissau	0.5	1,739	1,736	—	56	56	−50	106
Guyana	1.9	607	587	−3	24	28	12	16
Honduras	3.6	266	257	−4	28	32	39	−7
Madagascar	3.0	746	533	−34	−1	−33	−23	56
Malawi	1.7	324	398	20	65	45	41	3
Mali	1.3	581	332	−56	−14	42	34	8
Mauritania	1.7	357	339	−5	3	8	−2	10
Mozambique	5.2	1,593	1,325	−18	50	68	82	−14
Nicaragua	10.4	2,186	2,957	30	50	20	1	19
Niger	1.3	249	370	39	31	−8	6	−14
Senegal	4.1	224	278	22	55	33	13	20
Sierra Leone	1.2	640	556	−14	2	16	39	−23
Somalia	2.1	1,297	1,898	38	31	−7	−39	32
Sudan	16.5	1,250	4,084	118	61	−57	−56	−1
Tanzania	5.9	799	561	−35	4	39	23	16
Togo	1.2	181	222	20	31	10	22	−12
Uganda	2.3	241	1,145	156	88	−68	42	−110
Zaïre	10.4	322	640	68	62	−6	−60	54
Zambia	5.5	705	463	−42	3	44	−8	52
All countries	104.1	486	555	13	41	28	1	27
Average		595	779	21	44	23	11	11
Median		330	463	20	33	23	13	11

Source: IMF staff estimates.
[1]In percent of exports of goods and services.
[2]Index expressed in log normal terms.

In two of the cases (Bulgaria and Jordan), debt-servicing difficulties emerged only more recently. While the debt and debt-service indicators of these two countries deteriorated sharply, they were in 1992 at about the average of the first group (though moving in the opposite direction). Moreover, for Bulgaria, the share of debt owed to official bilateral creditors is less than 20 percent, and a resolution of its debt difficulties could be advanced through appropriate debt reduction by private creditors and steps to increase access to new flows from official bilateral sources. Jordan has been subject to a large structural shock, compounded by a loss of traditional grant financing, and thus faces somewhat greater difficulty in servicing its bilateral debt (Table A2).

Among the remaining countries, Côte d'Ivoire and Peru face particularly difficult situations. The stock of external debt is four to five times larger than annual exports, and most all of the debt is nonconcessional. For Peru, the increase in indebtedness from already high levels in 1986 is largely due to a capitalization of interest arrears. By contrast, Côte d'Ivoire maintained relations with official creditors in the context of successive reschedulings over most of the period under review. It thus obtained new financing as well as an interest rate reduction on previous rescheduled debt on a bilateral basis, but experienced a continued decline in exports. In both cases, available resources during the past two years have been directed largely to payments on multilateral and post-cutoff date debt.

Table 5. Low-Income Rescheduling Countries: Debt-Service Indicators by Country, 1986 and 1992[1]

(In percent of exports of goods and services)

	Total Scheduled Debt Service[2]		Actual Debt Service[2]		Scheduled Interest Payments	
	1986	1992	1986	1992	1986	1992
Angola	35	45	17	10	11	13
Benin	28	37	7	8	8	13
Bolivia	83	58	35	32	32	23
Burkina Faso	35	16	21	19	12	7
Central African Republic	22	25	17	10	8	9
Chad	12	12	10	1	6	5
Equatorial Guinea	51	47	33	42	17	20
Ethiopia	31	66	31	23	7	16
Gambia, The	49	11	24	11	15	2
Guinea	36	29	26	17	12	10
Guinea-Bissau	89	261	63	17	35	72
Guyana	81	60	20	47	33	23
Honduras	35	44	24	33	16	21
Madagascar	81	82	41	16	35	32
Malawi	63	25	43	25	20	8
Mali	47	46	25	14	12	10
Mauritania	45	39	26	20	16	14
Mozambique	247	160	4	24	78	52
Nicaragua	329	364	37	66	88	82
Niger	49	30	34	12	18	11
Senegal	37	24	26	13	13	9
Sierra Leone	89	32	31	16	33	15
Somalia	161	177	45	8	52	47
Sudan	108	325	31	19	61	209
Tanzania	70	43	17	15	25	18
Togo	30	21	27	4	10	8
Uganda	63	110	62	75	11	45
Zaïre	51	96	31	3	19	41
Zambia	95	64	32	48	38	26
Average	74	81	29	22	26	29
Total (weighted average)	63	64	28	20	23	24

Source: IMF staff estimates.
[1]Including the IMF.
[2]Including cash payments of arrears.

The Congo and Nigeria also face severe difficulty despite rapid export growth since 1986. In Cameroon, export declines have led to a rapid deterioration despite low initial indebtedness. These three countries have a high share in bilateral debt in total debt, and they would therefore be more dependent on this group of creditors.

Low-Income Rescheduling Countries

In contrast to the diversified experience of the lower middle-income countries over the past few years, the low-income rescheduling countries have seen little improvement in their debt situation and many have experienced a further marked deterioration. Most have been facing protracted balance of payments difficulties throughout the past decade.

Creditors have given increasing recognition to the special situation of these countries over the past years. Recent actions have gone a long way to help slow the pace of deterioration, although in most cases decisive improvements have yet to be achieved.

Main Features of Recent Experience

Three main features characterize developments since 1986. First, the combined noninterest current account deficit has risen steadily to nearly to $9 billion in 1992 (above 50 percent of annual exports of goods and services) (Table A3). This meant that these countries' capacity to service debt out of own resources has declined further both in nominal terms and relative to exports and that their overall

Table 6. Low-Income Rescheduling Countries: Structure of External Financing, 1992

(In percent of exports of goods and services)

	Noninterest Current Account Deficit (−: surplus)	Total Scheduled Debt Service[1]	Financing				
			Total	Grants	Disbursements	Exceptional	Other[2]
Angola	6	45	51	7	12	35	−3
Benin	41	37	78	15	14	29	19
Bolivia	17	58	75	29	49	26	−29
Burkina Faso	90	16	106	90	41	−3	−22
Central African Republic	81	25	106	69	48	15	−26
Chad	123	12	135	98	41	11	−15
Equatorial Guinea	80	47	127	105	36	5	−20
Ethiopia	93	66	159	79	43	43	−6
Gambia, The	19	11	30	21	11	—	−3
Guinea	38	29	67	18	29	12	8
Guinea-Bissau	150	261	411	200	215	244	−248
Guyana	9	60	69	1	8	13	47
Honduras	4	44	48	16	38	11	−16
Madagascar	22	82	104	24	28	66	−14
Malawi	88	25	113	35	22	—	56
Mali	66	46	112	78	37	32	−36
Mauritania	30	39	69	18	27	19	4
Mozambique	167	160	327	157	63	136	−29
Nicaragua	146	364	510	110	39	298	64
Niger	51	30	81	34	25	18	5
Senegal	18	24	42	21	22	11	−12
Sierra Leone	74	32	106	19	11	16	61
Somalia	276	177	453	187	107	169	−10
Sudan	207	325	532	59	123	306	44
Tanzania	116	43	159	55	25	28	50
Togo	21	21	42	15	5	17	5
Uganda	327	110	437	121	98	35	183
Zaïre	−3	96	93	2	2	93	−4
Zambia	54	64	118	54	24	16	24
Average	83	81	164	60	43	59	3

Source: IMF staff estimates.
[1]Including the IMF.
[2]Including other net capital flows and change in net reserves (increase −), including IMF purchases and disbursements.

need for external assistance has increased rapidly. Creditors and donors have responded by providing financial support on an increasing scale. Total financial assistance in the form of grants, new loan disbursements, and exceptional financing has been about as large as these countries' own earnings from exports of goods and services in every year since 1986 (Chart 2).

Creditors and donors have also recognized that financing on such a large scale would need to be provided on highly concessional terms. Thus, the proportion of financing in the form of grants has risen from around one fourth to one third (Table A3). New loans, including those from the multilateral institutions, have been provided on increasingly concessional terms. Finally, Paris Club creditors have been providing, since 1988, concessional reschedulings, first under Toronto terms and, since December 1991, on enhanced concessions.

Reflecting the increased concessionality of available financing, the average interest rate on debt obligations declined from about 5 percent in 1986 to less than 4½ percent in 1992.[4]

Second, the overall indebtedness of these countries remains extremely heavy and well above that of any other group of countries. It has increased rapidly over the past years, reaching over $100 billion at the end of 1992, over 550 percent of annual exports of goods and services. The combined scheduled interest ratio has remained broadly unchanged at some 24 percent despite the wide range of measures implemented by creditors to

---

[4]This decline in the average interest rate was achieved despite the substantial cancellations of official development assistance (ODA) debts, which, taken by themselves, resulted in an increase in the average interest rate on the stock remaining after cancellation.

Box 2. External Viability

There are no clear-cut criteria for assessing external viability because viability depends on the willingness of creditors to finance a country's current account deficits. Often, assessments of viability are based on market tests: access to spontaneous commercial borrowing, developments in secondary market prices of debt, or reliance on exceptional financing. A concept closely related to viability and central to an assessment of medium-term prospects is the sustainability of a country's external position, that is, the capacity of a country to finance a continuation of recent trends in the current account deficit without compromising its ability to meet debt-service payments.

Sustainability can be evaluated in terms of the evolution of ratios of debt and debt service to some domestic resource base, such as exports of goods and services. When these ratios are so high as to make a country unable to meet its contractual debt-service payments and resort to debt rescheduling, and the ratios can be expected to remain at high levels, the external position is unlikely to be sustainable; when debt-service ratios are falling and contractual obligations can be met, the external position is more likely to be sustainable.

In most of the rescheduling countries, conventional criteria for assessing external viability are not applicable because of the severity of these countries' initial debt problems, and the structure of their debt. This means that the traditional indicators of external viability, secondary market prices of commercial bank debt and access to spontaneous commercial borrowing, are either not applicable or so far out of reach as to be meaningless. Moreover, in many of these countries, debt burdens remain clearly excessive, and progress toward viability will entail a comprehensive restructuring of their debt.

In these circumstances, the appropriate measure of sustainability would be the extent to which scheduled debt-service ratios need to be reduced to eliminate exceptional financing, defined here as rescheduling of scheduled debt-service obligations and the accumulation of arrears to external creditors. While the need for debt reduction cannot be assessed on the basis of debt-service ratios alone, the experience of a wide range of countries suggests that actual debt-service ratios above 30 percent have been met only for short periods (though there were a few exceptions), and that ratios above 20 percent are difficult to sustain over the longer term, particularly for countries that have limited access to external financing that is not tied to imports of goods and services.

during this period, their share in total debt has declined slightly during the past few years following the cancellation of ODA debts, the effects of concessional reschedulings since 1988, and the shift towards grant financing.

The third and most striking feature of the situation of the low-income countries is the extent to which country circumstances differ. This underscores the difficulties of reaching generalized conclusions, especially since the aggregate picture is heavily dominated by a few large countries (Angola, Nicaragua, Sudan, Tanzania, and Zaïre account for nearly 50 percent of the debt of the low-income rescheduling countries). It also illustrates the need to approach individual country situations on a case-by-case basis.

Debt Burdens: Where Do We Stand?

The great diversity of country circumstances and experiences comes out clearly in Tables 4, 5, and 6 which provide country-specific information on the balance of payments structure and the composition of external financing in 1986 and 1992. (See also Table A4.) A detailed review of the experience of these countries and the interaction of the effects of internal policy adjustment, the external environment, and actions by creditors and donors is well beyond the scope of this paper.[5] Nevertheless, a number of broad conclusions emerge from the tables.

First, debt-service indicators have improved in nearly half of the rescheduling countries, but most continue to face unsustainable debt burdens. Debt stocks have increased in all but a few, even though the increased concessionality in new lending and in reschedulings has contributed to declines in scheduled interest ratios in nearly two thirds of the cases. These trends were particularly evident in countries that sustained their adjustment and reform efforts and obtained concessional financing in support of these efforts. Only two countries, however, have managed to graduate from Paris Club reschedulings (The Gambia and Malawi).

Second, a number of countries experienced a further, and often marked, increase in their debt burdens. Most of these countries faced very difficult initial balance of payments situations. For many, the situation was further exacerbated by uneven policy performance, often reflected in an accumulation of external arrears. These countries had, therefore, only limited access to new financing

reduce debt through ODA debt forgiveness and concessional reschedulings, and to increase the concessionality of remaining debt. About one fourth of the debt was owed to multilateral creditors, 20 percent to private creditors, and the remainder to official bilateral creditors. Although official bilateral creditors provided the largest share in financial flows

---

[5]For a detailed discussion of the experience of countries that implemented IMF-supported programs, see Susan Schadler and others, *Economic Adjustment in Low-Income Countries*, Occasional Paper, No. 106 (Washington: International Monetary Fund, September 1993).

Chart 3. Low-Income Rescheduling Countries: Structure of Scheduled Debt-Service Payments, 1992

(In percent of exports of goods and services)

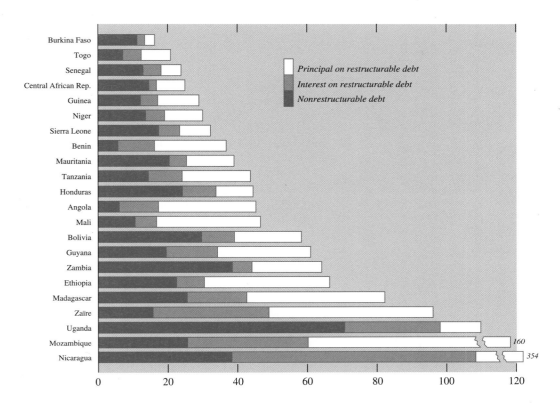

Source: IMF staff estimates.

on concessional terms, including concessional reschedulings. Some countries (such as Uganda) did sustain their adjustment efforts, but a sharp decline in exports more than offset the positive effects of adjustment and creditor actions.

Third, while scheduled debt-service burdens remain unsustainably high in most of the low-income rescheduling countries, actual payments on debt remained comparatively low as the result of debt reschedulings and, in some cases, the accumulation of arrears. Actual debt-service ratios remained typically lower than those of other low-income countries that have not rescheduled their debts. The actual cash impact of debt service was therefore in most cases markedly lower than scheduled debt service.

Finally, all of these countries obtained substantial net resource transfers (over and above actual debt-service payments) as demonstrated by their continuing large noninterest current account deficits. The noninterest current account balance (excluding grants) provides a measure of the net recourse to foreign savings, or, conversely, the net transfer of resources. As shown in Table 6, the average net transfers, measured in this fashion, amounted to 83 percent of countries' own export earnings in 1992. In a fourth of the cases, such net transfers exceeded own export earnings by substantial margins.

External debt and debt service have thus generally not been as burdensome as conventional debt measures would seem to indicate. From a cash-flow perspective, the strategy by official bilateral creditors of providing relief on debt-service obligations falling due has proven successful. It has also allowed creditors and donors to continue to provide substantial new financing, provided that the debtor countries maintained orderly relations through reschedulings. External viability has remained elusive, however, for nearly all of the low-income rescheduling countries: graduation from reschedulings would in most cases require continued successive reschedulings on a flow basis for many years.

It is for this reason that Paris Club creditors

Chart 4. Low-Income Rescheduling Countries: Structure of Payments on Nonrestructurable Debt, 1992
(In percent of exports of goods and services)

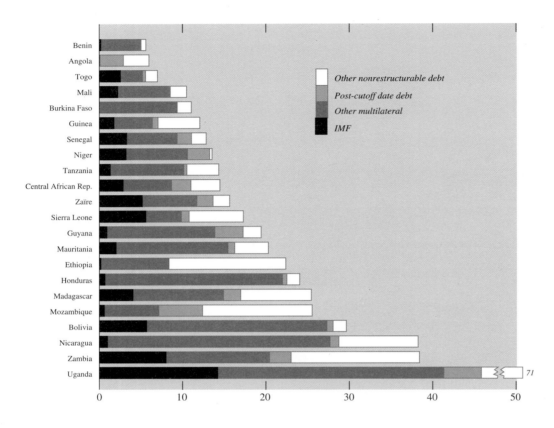

Source: IMF staff estimates.

decided that more definitive action on the stock of debt was needed for a durable solution to the debt problem of these countries. This renewed focus on medium-term debt-service burdens provides the low-income rescheduling countries with a clear prospect of graduation from the rescheduling process. The following sections examine the potential impact of such exit restructurings of the stock of debt by official bilateral creditors on the structure and the profile of debt-service obligations (Box 2).

Structure of Debt-Service Obligations

The extent of the debt-servicing difficulties currently faced by low-income rescheduling countries and the structure of debt-service payments for 1992 are illustrated in Chart 3 (Table A5). The chart distinguishes between payments on debts that cannot be restructured and debts that have been subject to debt restructurings. The first category includes debt to multilateral institutions (including the IMF),

post-cutoff date and short-term debts, as well as other debts that have been excluded from reschedulings, such as debt of the private sector, and obligations arising from previous Paris Club reschedulings on Toronto or enhanced concessional terms.[6] The category of restructurable debt includes pre-cutoff date debt to Paris Club creditors and other official bilateral and private creditors, including debts previously rescheduled on nonconcessional terms.

Chart 3 also shows the extent to which debt-service payments are related to debts that cannot be restructured and are therefore not amenable to actions by official bilateral creditors. Chart 4 provides further detail on the structure of these obligations and, in particular payments to multilateral

---

[6]The subordination strategy of Paris Club creditors regarding pre-cutoff and post-cutoff date debts and their policies regarding debt-service obligations arising from previous reschedulings on concessional terms are described in Section III.

Chart 5. Low-Income Rescheduling Countries: Structure of Payments on Restructurable Debt, 1992
(In percent of exports of goods and services)

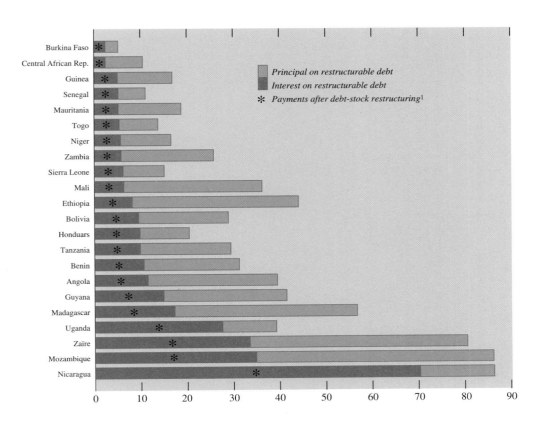

Sources: Chart 3; and IMF staff estimates.
[1]Assuming a stock-of-debt restructuring that incorporates a reduction of 50 percent in net present value terms, as currently implemented by the Paris Club on a flow basis.

institutions. Obligations to the IMF remain a relatively small fraction of total debt payments in all but a few cases (such as Uganda and Zambia), but a number of countries face heavy debt obligations to other multilateral institutions. For Guyana, Madagascar, Mauritania, and Zambia, the debt-service ratio to multilaterals (excluding the IMF) exceeds 10 percent, and for Bolivia, Honduras, Nicaragua, and Uganda, the ratio ranges from 15 percent to 25 percent. By contrast, current obligations on post-cutoff date debts to official bilateral creditors remain very small in all cases, reflecting the highly concessional nature of these debts.

Debt-Stock Operations for Low-Income Countries

The new menu of enhanced concessions agreed by Paris Club creditors in December 1991 provides for the possibility of a stock-of-debt operation pro-

vided certain conditions are met. This subsection provides an assessment of the potential impact of stock-of-debt operations by official bilateral creditors.

Impact of Debt-Stock Restructurings

Countries have returned to the Paris Club time after time because of continuing heavy debt-service burdens. This is illustrated for 1992 by Charts 3 and 5. As can be seen from these charts, for most countries, the bulk of scheduled debt-service payments arises on restructurable debt; this results mainly from previous reschedulings on nonconcessional terms that had relatively short grace and repayment periods. A durable exit from the rescheduling process can therefore only be achieved by a fundamental restructuring of the total stock of restructurable debt. As described in more detail in Section III, Paris Club creditors have recently established a broad framework for action on the stock of pre-

Table 7. Selected Low-Income Rescheduling Countries: Effect of Debt-Stock Operations[1,2]

(In percent of exports of goods and service)

	Scheduled Debt Service			Debt Service After a Hypothetical 50 Percent Stock-of-Debt Operation	
	Nonrestructurable debt[3]	Restructurable debt[4]		Restructurable debt	Total
		Principal	Interest	(4) =	(5) =
	(1)	(2)	(3)	50 percent of (3)	(1) + (4)
Angola	6	28	11	6	12
Benin	6	21	10	5	11
Bolivia	30	19	9	5	34
Burkina Faso	11	3	2	1	12
Central African Republic	14	8	2	1	16
Ethiopia	22	36	8	4	26
Guinea	12	12	5	2	14
Guyana	19	26	15	7	27
Honduras	24	11	10	5	29
Madagascar	25	40	17	9	34
Mali	10	30	6	3	14
Mauritania	20	14	5	3	23
Mozambique	25	99	35	17	43
Nicaragua	38	256	70	35	73
Niger	13	11	6	3	16
Senegal	13	6	5	3	15
Sierra Leone	17	9	6	3	20
Tanzania	14	20	10	5	19
Togo	7	8	5	3	10
Uganda	71	12	27	14	84
Zaïre	16	47	33	17	32
Zambia	38	20	6	3	41

Sources: Table A5; and IMF staff estimates.

[1]Totals may not add due to rounding.

[2]The debt-service structure for 1992 is broadly representative of the debt-service profile over the medium term. Liberia, Somalia, and Sudan are excluded due to data limitations.

[3]Includes short-term debt and other debt that have been excluded explicitly or implicitly from rescheduling, such as private sector debts as well as debt service from previous concessional rescheduling on Toronto terms and on enhanced concessions.

[4]Includes pre-cutoff date debt to Paris Club, other official bilateral, and private creditors.

cutoff date debt through the adoption of the menu of enhanced concessions, although the terms of the stock operation have yet to be determined.

A restructuring of the debt stock with long repayment periods would, by reducing principal payments, contribute significantly toward bringing debt-service profiles more in line with countries' underlying payments capacities. A restructuring alone without concessions would, however, not reduce scheduled interest payments. It would thus leave most of the countries concerned with debt-service burdens that would offer little prospect of a durable graduation from reschedulings. Scheduled interest payments will also need to be reduced to achieve a debt-service profile consistent with external viability. This would require a debt-stock reduction or equivalent interest concessions.

The immediate impact of a possible stock-of-debt reduction on debt-service payments in 1992 can be seen in Chart 5 and Table 7. A restructuring of the

stock of debt into a mortgage-type repayment schedule would initially eliminate or reduce scheduled principal payments to a very small fraction of the restructured debt stock. It would also reduce scheduled interest payments by the amount of the net present value reduction of the debt stock. For example, if creditors applied to the stock of debt the 50 percent net present value reduction currently implemented by the Paris Club on a flow basis, payments on the restructured stock would be reduced to about half of the currently scheduled level of interest payments.[7] For most countries,

---

[7]Two important assumptions underlie this assessment of payments due after a stock-of-debt reduction. First, other official bilateral and private creditors are assumed to provide comparable treatment. Second, interest on ODA debts is not reduced under the current Paris Club menu, and if this was also the case for stock operations, there would be a correspondingly smaller reduction in scheduled interest payments.

such a hypothetical stock of debt reduction would reduce total payments on restructurable debts to well below 5 percent of exports of goods and services.

Degree of Reduction

In most cases, debt reductions by Paris Club creditors beyond 50 percent would make only small additional contributions to improvements in the debt-service profile. For the bulk of cases where a net present value reduction by 50 percent would, based on the 1992 position, lower debt payments on restructured debt to 5 percent of exports, a move to a 75 percent reduction, for example, would result in an additional reduction of debt-service ratios by only 2½ percentage points.

A number of countries, however, face exceptionally difficult debt situations and their debt problems will not be resolved by a 50 percent net present value reduction (e.g., Guyana, Madagascar, Mozambique, Nicaragua, Uganda, and Zambia, in particular).[8] Substantially deeper debt reductions will be required to reduce debt-service payments to managable levels, even with ambitious and sustained adjustment efforts by the countries themselves.

In some of these cases, the solution to the debt problem lies largely outside the Paris Club, because the bulk of restructurable debt is owed to creditors that do not participate in the Paris Club, including the former Soviet Union. As reported in Section III, some of the non-Paris Club creditors have already shown in a number of cases considerable flexibility in adopting innovative approaches, including very comprehensive debt reductions. Similarly flexible responses will be required for other debtors.

Sustainability

The discussion so far has concentrated on debt-service obligations in 1992. The conclusions hold, and indeed are reinforced, for future debt-service obligations. For restructured debt, under a graduated repayment schedule (as currently employed under the menu of enhanced concessions), debt-service obligations would increase at an annual rate of only 3 percent in nominal terms (the first panel of Chart 6). With nominal export growth expected to be higher (which would be consistent with little or no growth in real terms), the debt-service burden on such debt would thus be projected to decline steadily over time (as illustrated in the second panel of Chart 6). For existing nonrestructurable debt, the

---

[8]This also holds for Liberia, Somalia, and Sudan, which are not included here because of data limitations.

Chart 6. Hypothetical Debt-Service Profile and Export Growth After Debt Restructuring[1]

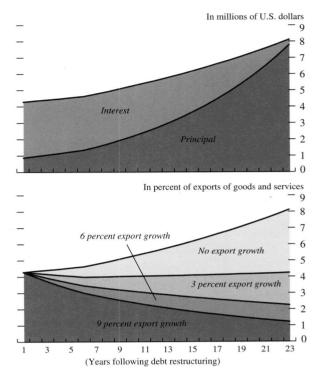

Source: IMF staff estimates.

[1]Export growth in nominal terms. Assuming a restructuring of $100 million in debt on the terms currently applied under enhanced concessional terms on a flow basis, with a reduction of 50 percent in net present value terms; a market rate of 9 percent; an equal distribution over the debt-reduction and debt-service-reduction options; and initial exports of $100 million. Note that for the debt-service-reduction option in the current Paris Club menu, which effects the net present value reduction through concessional interest rates, interest rates are reduced by more than half. This has been offset in the current menu by eliminating the grace period for this option in order to arrive at broadly equivalent cash payments under the debt-reduction and debt-servicing-reduction options.

same conclusion holds. Both official bilateral post-cutoff date debt and multilateral debt have increasingly been provided on concessional terms and for longer maturities. Hence, no pronounced hump of debt-service payments is expected. In real terms, therefore, the debt-service burden on this debt should also decline over time. Provided new disbursements are provided on appropriately concessional terms, as is discussed further below, and reasonable export growth is achieved, the overall debt-service picture as a result of stock of debt operations should improve from the illustrative snapshot provided of the impact in 1992.

To be successful, debt-stock operations must ensure that debt-service obligations are brought to

Chart 7. Low-Income Rescheduling Countries: Debt-Service and Direct Financial Assistance, 1992
(In percent of exports of goods and services)

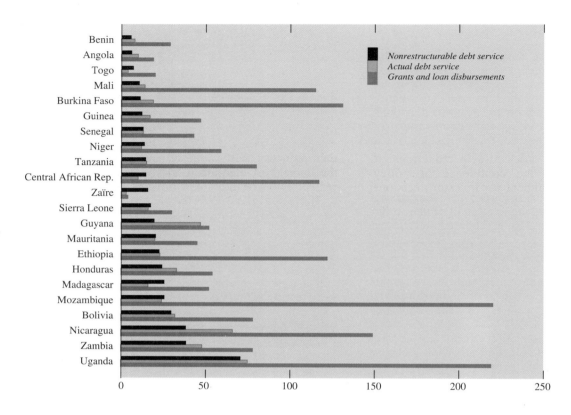

Source: IMF staff estimates.

levels that are sustainable over the medium term. This underlines the importance of a primary focus on the debt-service profile resulting from debt-stock restructurings rather than other debt indicators. A comprehensive assessment would also need to be based on detailed country-specific medium-term scenarios to take into account the wide variations among countries as regards the stage of the adjustment process and, more particularly, their export prospects and ability to attract new financing.

The debt profile resulting from a stock-of-debt operation would typically require higher payments on restructurable debts than countries are currently making. This reflects large immediate cash-flow relief provided under most current reschedulings. This raises the question whether countries would be able to meet the higher payments following a stock-of-operation or whether they would continue to require additional cash-flow relief.

For most countries that had effective rescheduling agreements in 1992, payments resulting from a hypothetical stock operation would, however, not

be significantly higher than total payments actually made in 1992. This is due to two factors. Both are related to the resumption of regular relations with official creditors. First, many countries were required to clear arrears on Paris Club debts that are not normally covered by reschedulings. These were one-time payments typically associated with a return to reschedulings after a period during which arrears accumulated. Second, in some cases, very comprehensive Paris Club reschedulings provided room for a regularization of relations with multilateral institutions. The same approach will be required for countries that are currently without effective rescheduling agreements and are accumulating arrears on nonrestructurable debts. In these cases, the need for cash payments on nonrestructurable arrears could add significantly to the actual debt burden during the initial years.

The phased approach to debt reduction, as currently implemented by the Paris Club, takes account of these initial difficulties. It assists countries in regularizing relations, establishing a record of performance, and adjusting into the more inflexible payments stream that will result from a restructuring of the debt stock. At the same time, creditors continue to review the possibility of earlier exit restructurings on a case-by-case basis.[9] Earlier operations would be particularly relevant for countries that have already established a record of sustained implementation of comprehensive programs of adjustment and reform, and have maintained orderly relations with creditors in the context of existing rescheduling agreements. In such cases, timely action on the stock of debt would provide debtors with clear assurances that official bilateral creditors are prepared to provide definitive exit restructurings through stock-of-debt reductions. It would thus improve the confidence of policy makers and the environment for investor decisions in these countries. It would also help eliminate the uncertainties that currently cloud assessments of the prospects for external viability.

Finally, as noted earlier, the rescheduling countries remain heavily dependent on continued direct financial assistance in the form of grants and new disbursements from official sources. As illustrated in Chart 7, these new flows are typically several times larger than actual debt-service payments. The high level of grants and the concessionality of debt in many of these countries raises the question of whether donors would continue to provide grants and concessional financing on the scale experienced in the past, once normal relations with creditors are re-established and the debt burden is reduced to a sustainable level (given concessional terms). For most of the countries under review, the magnitude of resource requirements severely circumscribes the potential role of debt-creating flows. External viability would be out of reach if financing needs had to be met exclusively by debt on market-related terms. Moreover, even marginal changes in the level of new financial support could have serious repercussions on these countries' ability to remain current on their debt obligations. The adequacy of debt reduction will therefore need to be assessed in the context of medium-term scenarios that give a realistic view of likely new flows.

These considerations also underscore the need for debtor countries to reinforce and broaden their efforts to improve domestic savings and growth performance, through continued structural change. The experience of countries that have recently re-established normal relations with creditors demonstrates that a successful resolution of debt problems requires not only actions on existing debt but must be based on sustained implementation of appropriate policies. These include policies that will attract foreign investment and reduce reliance on debt-creating flows in order to bring about a decisive strengthening of the overall balance of payments position over the medium term.

---

[9]This was noted in the July 1993 Tokyo Summit communiqué of the Group of Seven major industrial countries.

III

Recent Developments in Debt Restructurings by Official Bilateral Creditors

This section provides information on recent debt restructurings by official bilateral creditors. The first part reports on recent debt renegotiations of official bilateral debt in the multilateral Paris Club framework; the second summarizes information on recent debt renegotiations involving other official bilateral creditors; and the third describes recent debt forgiveness initiatives implemented by a number of creditors on a bilateral basis.[10]

Paris Club Rescheduling Agreements

In recent years, Paris Club debt reschedulings have been increasingly adapted to the divergent experiences of different groups of rescheduling countries. This reflects a renewed focus by creditors on approaches that would promote debtor countries' graduation from the rescheduling process. Two developments stand out.

First, the number of countries requiring cash-flow relief from Paris Club creditors has been declining over the past two years for the first time since the early 1980s, as an increasing number of *middle-income rescheduling countries* has been making substantial progress toward resolving their debt problems. While only six countries had managed to graduate from Paris Club reschedulings during the 1980s, eight countries (all in the middle-income category) have done so over the past two years, and a number of others can be expected to do so at the end of their current Paris Club consolidation periods. Notwithstanding this progress, however, a few lower middle-income countries continue to face very difficult situations.

Second, in sharp contrast to the broadly favorable prospects for many of the middle-income countries, the debt situation of the *low-income rescheduling countries* has remained arduous despite repeated reschedulings and re-reschedulings, stretching back, in several cases, over the past ten or more years. In response to the protracted difficulties,

Paris Club creditors adopted in December 1991 the new menu of "enhanced concessions" in reschedulings for these countries.[11] This new approach recognizes that a durable solution to the debt problem of the most heavily indebted low-income countries would require both a higher degree of concessionality in reschedulings and a fundamental restructuring of the stock of pre-cutoff date debt.

The new menu provides for a *two-stage approach*. The first consists of continued flow reschedulings of debt service falling due, and the amounts consolidated are reduced by 50 percent (in net present value terms). In the second stage, after a period of three to four years, creditors will consider the stock of debt, provided that a number of conditions are met, notably full implementation of rescheduling agreements and continued implementation of IMF-supported programs. The terms of the debt-stock operation have yet to be determined, but, as set out in the previous section, this new focus by Paris Club creditors on a definitive resolution of the debt-servicing difficulties through a stock-of-debt operation provides low-income rescheduling countries that are implementing adjustment programs with a clear prospect of graduation from the rescheduling process.

Table A6 summarizes the current status of the 58 rescheduling countries and lists the expiration date of their current or last consolidation period. The grouping into low- and lower-middle income countries reflects the terms these countries have obtained from Paris Club creditors.[12] The recent evolution of Paris Club rescheduling terms for these different groups of countries are summarized in Table A7. Chart 8 shows the resulting shift in repayments pro-

---

[10]Multilateral official debt renegotiations that took place through 1990 and Paris Club general practices are described in Michael G. Kuhn, with Jorge P. Guzman, *Multilateral Official Debt Rescheduling: Recent Experience*, World Economic and Financial Surveys (Washington: International Monetary Fund, November 1990).

[11]The new menu has yet to find a commonly accepted name. This paper uses the term "enhanced concessions." The menu has also been called "enhanced Toronto terms." While the term "Trinidad terms" has been used by some, the term has been misleading, since Trinidad terms refer to an earlier proposal by the then Chancellor of the Exchequer Major in Trinidad (calling for a flat two thirds reduction of the stock of pre-cutoff date debt). This proposal was not implemented, though the Paris Club menu incorporates some of its features.

[12]The determination of eligibility for concessional terms has been made on a case-by-case basis. The country classification differs from those used by the Organization for Economic Cooperation and Development (OECD) and the World Bank.

Chart 8. Average Repayment Schedule, 1985–
June 1993[1]

(In percent of total debt service covered)[2]

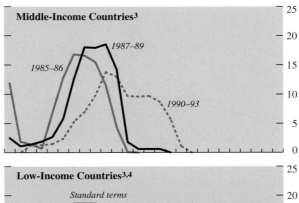

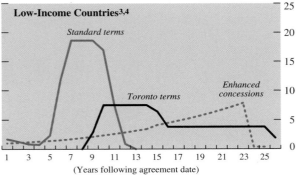

(Years following agreement date)

Sources: Debt-rescheduling agreements; and IMF staff estimates.
[1]Excludes consolidated debt service on ODA loans.
[2]Excludes interest on the rescheduling.
[3]See Table 1 for definitions of groups.
[4]For a description of these terms, see Table A7.

files on rescheduled debt for the low- and middle-income countries.

Rescheduling Agreements in 1992–93

Twenty-eight rescheduling agreements were concluded during 1992 and the first half of 1993 (Table A10). This brings the total number of Paris Club reschedulings since 1976 to 212, involving a total of 58 debtor countries and debt-service obligations amounting to $237 billion (Table 8).[13] These recent agreements illustrate the continuing evolution of Paris Club rescheduling practices and the variety of terms and coverage creditors have used in tailoring debt reschedulings to the circumstances of individual countries. Twelve agreements involved middle-income countries. Of these, the agreements with Costa Rica and Guatemala covered arrears only and were considered exit reschedulings. The rescheduling agreements for Cameroon, Ecuador, Jamaica, Jordan, Morocco, and Peru incorporated longer maturities (applied since September 1990 in reschedulings for heavily indebted lower middle-income countries) and provided for comprehensive coverage of debt service. Argentina, Brazil, and Bulgaria obtained reschedulings on standard terms, incorporating, in the former two cases, a graduated repayments schedule with shorter grace periods but longer overall repayment periods. Official bilateral creditors also concluded a comprehensive rescheduling agreement with the Russian Federation. The remaining 16 rescheduling agreements involved low-income countries, all of which obtained enhanced concessions with typically comprehensive coverage.

Over the past year, there has been a marked intensification of the trend toward *multiyear consolidations* on the basis of multiyear IMF arrangements. The consolidations for Argentina, Jamaica, and Peru covered a period of three years (in line with arrangements under the IMF's extended Fund facility). Similarly, the consolidation periods for Benin, Burkina Faso, Ethiopia, Honduras, Mali, Mauritania, Mozambique, Tanzania, Togo, and Zambia all ranged between two and three years. In line with standard Paris Club practice, multiyear consolidations were tranched, with effectiveness of the second (or third) tranche linked, inter alia, to approval by the IMF Board of subsequent annual arrangements under the enhanced structural adjustment facility or structural adjustment facility or annual reviews under extended Fund facility arrangements, or under rights accumulation programs (Sierra Leone and Zambia).[14]

The move toward longer consolidation periods has contributed to a reduction in the frequency of Paris Club reschedulings over the recent past and an increase in the number of countries with rescheduling agreements in effect. Despite this, at the end of June 1993, only 20 of the 44 countries that require continued cash-flow relief had agreements in effect. Some countries are expected to obtain reschedulings in the near future on the basis of new IMF arrangements. In a number of other cases, discus-

[13]Table A9 provides a complete listing of Paris Club rescheduling agreements since 1976. The starting date of 1976 is to some extent arbitrary, since multilateral official debt reschedulings through the Paris Club date back to 1956, although the pattern of reschedulings has changed considerably. The ten countries that concluded reschedulings during 1956–75 all resumed normal relations with creditors after a brief series of reschedulings. Most of the countries that have rescheduled since 1976, however, have remained in a rescheduling situation almost without interruption. Both creditors and debtors thus frequently refer to specific exercises by the numbers as indicated in Table A9.

[14]For information on the various facilities of the IMF and how they work, see *Financial Organization and Operations of the IMF*, IMF Pamphlet Series, No. 45 (Washington: International Monetary Fund, 2d ed., 1991).

Table 8. Amount Consolidated and Number of Renegotiations of Official Bilateral Debt, 1986–June 1993[1]

	1986	1987	1988	1989	1990	1991	1992	Jan.–June 1993
(Amount consolidated in billions of U.S. dollars)								
Low-income countries	9.2	1.5	1.2	3.0	2.8	0.9	2.6	0.8
Under Toronto terms	—	—	0.5	2.0	2.8	0.2	—	—
Under enhanced concessions	—	—	—	—	—	0.8	2.6	0.8
Middle-income countries	3.9	23.9	8.2	15.6	13.7	72.6[2]	16.9	16.7
Cumulative total amount consolidated[3]	56.0	81.5	90.9	109.5	126.0	199.5	219.1	236.5
(Number of reschedulings)								
Low-income countries	12	7	9	13	10	4	11	5
Middle-income countries	4	10	6	11	8	12	7	5
Cumulative total number of reschedulings[3]	94	111	126	150	168	184	202	212
Cumulative total number of rescheduling countries[3]	40	42	43	50	52	55	56	58

Sources: Debt-rescheduling agreements; and IMF staff estimates.
[1]For country group definitions, see Table A6.
[2]Includes a total of $57.8 billion of debt restructured in the agreements with Egypt and Poland.
[3]Cumulative since 1976.

sions on an adjustment program that would allow the regularization of relations are still at an early stage. Finally, a few of the rescheduling countries have been accumulating arrears to creditors for several years.

Coverage and Subordination Strategy

Official bilateral creditors have been assisting countries with debt-servicing difficulties not only through debt rescheduling, but also through the provision of new financial assistance. For countries that require cash-flow relief on existing obligations, Paris Club creditors have been implementing a ` strategy of subordinating "old" loans to "new" credits in order to preserve the flow of new credits.

The heart of this subordination strategy has been the maintenance, since May 1984, of the *cutoff date* in all rescheduling agreements with IMF member countries seeking successive rescheduling. The cutoff date is established in the first rescheduling agreement. Debt-service payments on old (pre-cutoff date) loans are eligible to be consolidated under the first and subsequent agreements, whereas payments due on new (post-cutoff date) loans are not covered and must be serviced on schedule.

The strategy has been crucial to the continuation of both direct financial assistance (including assistance on concessional terms) and support in the form of guarantees or insurance for exports or other credits extended by the private sector. The recent innovations in debt reschedulings have reinforced

this strategy as concessional reschedulings have maintained the clear distinction between old claims and new claims. The subordination strategy has been applied strictly in all recent Paris Club reschedulings to payments falling due over the consolidation period. Creditors have also required that any arrears on post-cutoff date debts be settled promptly, often as a precondition for a new rescheduling.

Paris Club creditors have also continued their policy of excluding from rescheduling *short-term debt* falling due during the consolidation period. The maintenance of, or increases in, short-term credit lines by official export credit agencies has been an essential element in the financial support for countries implementing adjustment programs. In consequence, debtor countries have generally not requested a consolidation of current debt service on these debts. However, creditors have agreed, on an exceptional basis, to consolidate arrears on short-term debts for first-time reschedulers or in subsequent reschedulings when short-term arrears turned out to be much larger than had been earlier estimated.

Another aspect of the strategy is the treatment of *private sector claims* that are not guaranteed by the debtor government. During the early 1980s, these claims were generally included in the consolidation, except for countries with convertible currencies through their membership in currency unions. During the past years, however, these claims have usually been excluded, and exclusion of private sector debt has now become the norm rather than the exception.

Creditors have agreed to comprehensive coverage of other pre-cutoff date debts. When the payments capacity of the debtor country was severely constrained, creditors had already moved toward 100 percent coverage of interest and principal payments on original maturities (not arising from previous reschedulings), including arrears. In many cases, debt service arising from previously rescheduled debt (PRD) accounts for the largest share of debt obligations falling due, reflecting in part the terms of previous consolidations. As debt-servicing difficulties persisted for many of the repeat reschedulers, it became increasingly necessary to re-reschedule previously rescheduled debt, especially for the low- and some lower middle-income countries.

This trend toward increasingly comprehensive coverage has been accompanied by finer distinctions among various subcategories of debts arising from previous reschedulings and re-reschedulings. The agreements have typically consolidated 100 percent of interest and principal payments (as well as arrears, where necessary) of debts covered under the agreements. In most cases, creditors have, however, excluded from coverage payments arising from the previous or past two reschedulings. It has also been standard practice to exclude from reschedulings debt service arising from previous reschedulings on concessional terms for low-income countries.

Evolution of Rescheduling Terms for Low-Income Countries

Official bilateral creditors have provided cash-flow relief to a large number of low-income countries. These countries account for about half of the countries that have obtained Paris Club reschedulings but have been involved in two thirds of the rescheduling agreements. Generally, the reschedulings for these countries were more comprehensive in coverage than those for other debtors. However, given the protracted nature of their balance of payments problems, many countries experienced serious difficulties in adhering to the repayment schedules from previous agreements. Creditors increasingly recognized that the repeated application of standard terms over a long period did not provide an adequate response to the medium-term debt-servicing difficulties of the poorest and most heavily indebted countries.

Toronto Terms

In late 1988, creditors took a first step toward reducing the future debt-service burden resulting from successive reschedulings. Agreement was reached to implement a menu of options, "Toronto terms." This menu includes elements of debt and debt-service reduction (Table A7). During 1988–91, these concessional rescheduling terms were applied in 28 rescheduling agreements, involving 20 debtor countries and a total amount consolidated of some $6 billion. Reschedulings under Toronto terms provided an average grant element of well over 20 percent for nonconcessional debt. There was also a slight increase in the concessionality over time as more creditors chose the most concessional option. These reschedulings provided substantial debt relief. Together with continued flows of concessional new financing, they led to an improvement in the debt situation of a number of low-income countries.

Creditors increasingly recognized, however, that the vast majority of low-income rescheduling countries required more far-reaching concessions for a sustained improvement in their debt situation. They also recognized that a continuation of the approach—covering only those debt-service payments falling due during a limited consolidation period—would in many cases require a long series of repeated reschedulings to bring about a substantial reduction in the debt-service burden over the medium term.

The main starting point for discussions on more far-reaching debt relief for the low-income countries was the U.K. "Trinidad terms" proposal of September 1990. The discussions intensified after the Heads of State and Governments of the Group of Seven at the London Summit in July 1991 agreed that additional debt relief measures were needed for the poorest countries on a case-by-case basis and called on the Paris Club to continue its discussions on how such measures could be implemented. The IMF's Interim Committee and Development Committee in October 1991 further emphasized the importance of these deliberations.

The New Menu—Enhanced Concessions

In December 1991, Paris Club creditors reached agreement on the modalities of implementing deeper concessions for the low-income countries through a new menu of options that was designed to allow creditors to provide concessional debt relief while taking account of their varying institutional and budgetary constraints. The new menu contained a number of innovative features, including an approach to debt restructuring in two stages, which combine the flexibility of the flow approach during the adjustment period with the possibility of a later stock-of-debt operation that could provide a definitive resolution of the debt problem.

This new menu of "*enhanced concessions*" provides for a 50 percent reduction (in net present value terms) of debt service consolidated on non-ODA debts through two main options. Under the first option, *debt reduction*, 50 percent of the debt service consolidated is canceled; the remainder is rescheduled at market interest rates over 23 years with a graduated repayments schedule including a grace period of 6 years. Under the second option, *debt-service reduction*, consolidated debt service is rescheduled at reduced interest rates to reduce the present value by 50 percent. Principal repayments are graduated over a 23-year period with no grace period. The cash-flow implications under these two main options are broadly equal. There is also a variant of the debt-service reduction option that combines a lesser reduction of interest rates with a *partial capitalization of moratorium interest*, which also provides a 50 percent present value reduction.[15] Consolidated debt service on ODA credits is rescheduled over 30 years, including a grace period of 12 years, at concessional ODA interest rates, entailing a substantial reduction in the net present value of debt. Finally, the menu also includes an option providing for *long maturities* but without concessions and provides for the possibility of debt conversions on a bilateral and voluntary basis.

The rescheduling agreements based on the new menu contain the provision that Paris Club creditors would be willing to consider the matter of the *stock of debt* after a period of 3–4 years. Creditors also continue to review the possibility of earlier stock operations. For such consideration, the debtor country must have fully implemented the earlier rescheduling agreements, obtained comparable debt relief from other creditors, and continued appropriate arrangements with the IMF. Creditors have emphasized that the application of concessions was to be limited to those poorest countries not in a position to service debts on commercial terms. The Agreed Minutes for concessional rescheduling refer, in particular, to very heavy debt-service obligations in conjunction with very low per capita income, chronic balance of payments problems, and the implementation of a strong adjustment program.

An important feature of the menu of enhanced concessions is its *graduated repayment schedule*, which avoids the humps at the end of the grace period of repayment terms under conventional reschedulings. Under this new schedule, debt-service payments on restructured debt in nominal terms increase at an annual rate of about 3 percent. With exports projected to increase at higher rates in nominal terms (which would be consistent with little or no growth in real terms), the debt-service

burden on restructured debt could be expected to decline steadily over time. This would mean that these debts by themselves should not become cause for serious debt-servicing difficulties.

Implementation of the New Menu

To date, all 17 low-income countries that have concluded rescheduling agreements with the Paris Club since December 1991 have benefited from enhanced concessions (Table A10). Coverage of pre-cutoff date debts under the reschedulings was typically comprehensive, including arrears on debt covered by the agreement. For repeat reschedulers, debt service arising from previous reschedulings on nonconcessional terms was also covered. In a few cases, the agreements also provided cash-flow relief on debt service from previous reschedulings on Toronto terms, but without further concessions and over shorter repayment periods.

In these agreements on enhanced concessions, creditors agreed to cover all obligations due on pre-cutoff date debt (i.e., original maturities not arising from previous reschedulings) for a total of nearly $2 billion. In addition, creditors agreed to consolidate $2.4 billion of $2.7 billion due on previously rescheduled debt. This brought the total amount consolidated on enhanced concessions to $4.4 billion (close to the total $5.5 billion consolidated in 28 reschedulings on Toronto terms between late 1988 and late 1991). The average debt reduction under enhanced concessions has been about 46 percent, thus involving a debt reduction of about $2 billion in net present value terms.[16] The reschedulings reduced actual payments on pre-cutoff date debt to some 6 percent of amounts due. Taking into account some $0.2 billion in moratorium interest, actual debt-service payments to Paris Club creditors were reduced to about $0.5 billion on an annual basis. In addition, countries made payments of about $0.5 billion due on post-cutoff date debt (Table 9).

Rescheduling Terms for Middle-Income Countries

The rescheduling terms for middle-income countries have depended on the country's income level and extent of indebtedness. The coverage of debts rescheduled has reflected these countries' wide variety of circumstances.

---

[15]No interest accrues on capitalized moratorium interest.

[16]The average debt reduction on non-ODA debt is less than 50 percent because the menu also contains a nonconcessional option. In May of 1993, the U.S. administration announced that it would request congressional authorization and budgetary appropriations to allow the United States to choose a concessional option in Paris Club reschedulings on enhanced concessions.

Table 9. Low-Income Rescheduling Countries: Amounts Due and Consolidated Under Enhanced Concessions, 1991–June 1993[1,2]

(In millions of U.S. dollars)

	Arrears as of Start of Consolidation	Debt Service Falling Due During Consolidation Period	Total
Pre-cutoff date debt			
Debt service due	1,895	2,848	4,744
Not previously rescheduled	1,047	989	2,036
Previously rescheduled	849	1,859	2,708
Consolidated	1,752	2,697	4,449
Not previously rescheduled	1,045	989	2,034
Previously rescheduled	707	1,708	2,415
Amount to be paid as percent of amount due	(7.6)	(5.3)	(6.2)
Not previously rescheduled	(—)	(—)	(—)
Previously rescheduled	(16.6)	(8.1)	(10.8)
Memorandum items			
Moratorium interest	—	221	221
Post-cutoff date debt	214	278	492
Total debt service to be paid after consolidation	357	650	1,007

Sources: Debt-rescheduling agreements; and IMF staff estimates.
[1]Totals may not add due to rounding.
[2]Includes reschedulings for Benin, Bolivia, Burkina Faso, Equatorial Guinea, Ethiopia, Guinea, Guyana, Honduras, Mali, Mauritania, Mozambique, Nicaragua, Sierra Leone, Tanzania, Togo, Uganda, and Zambia.

Lower Middle-Income Countries

In September 1990, Paris Club creditors agreed on a new set of rescheduling terms for lower middle-income countries. The new terms extended the standard maturities of 10 years (with 5 or 6 years' grace) to 15 years (with a maximum grace period of 8 years) for commercial credits; and up to 20 years (with a maximum grace period of 10 years) for ODA credits. The agreements also specified that ODA debt would be rescheduled at concessional interest rates. While this had been the practice of most creditors in the past, it was not required under previous agreements. Eligibility for these terms is determined on a case-by-case basis taking account of the level of per capita income, the share of external debt owed to bilateral creditors in relation to that owed to commercial banks, and a number of indicators of the severity of the countries' indebtedness. An innovative feature of the new terms was the provision for debt conversions on a voluntary basis in the form of debt-for-equity, debt-for-aid, debt-for-nature, and other debt-for-local-currency operations.[17]

Repayment terms applied to rescheduled current

maturities of nonconcessional previously rescheduled debt have generally been the same as those granted on original maturities and creditors also continued to grant the same repayment terms for rescheduled arrears. Coverage of debts for the middle-income countries reflected these countries' wide variety of circumstances. In two cases (Costa Rica and Guatemala), a rescheduling of arrears was sufficient; others required more comprehensive cash-flow relief.

Since 1991, there have been 13 reschedulings incorporating the longer maturities for lower middle-income countries. These covered $9.6 billion of $10 billion due on original maturities and $6.2 billion of $8.7 billion due on previously rescheduled debt.[18] After taking into account moratorium interest payments of $1.3 billion, actual debt service of these countries on Paris Club pre-cutoff date debt was reduced to $4.2 billion compared with $18.7 billion debt-service obligations falling due in that

---

[17]In practice, creditors have limited the use of swaps to the higher of $10 million or 10 percent of consolidated commercial credits, but no restrictions have been set on ODA and direct government loans.

---

[18]Côte d'Ivoire, Dominican Republic, Jamaica, Nigeria, Peru, and the Philippines in 1991; Cameroon, Ecuador, Jordan, and Morocco in 1992; and Guatemala, Jamaica, and Peru in 1993. Congo, El Salvador, Honduras, Morocco, and Poland benefited from the longer maturities during 1990, after these repayment terms were adopted by Paris Club creditors in September of that year. The debt-restructuring and debt-reduction agreements with Egypt and Poland are excluded from these figures.

Table 10. Lower Middle-Income Rescheduling Countries: Amounts Due and Consolidated, 1991–June 1993[1]

(In millions of U.S. dollars)

	Arrears as of Start of Consolidation	Debt Service Falling Due During Consoli- dation Period	Total
Pre-cutoff date debt			
Debt service due	9,320	9,406	18,726
Not previously rescheduled	6,209	3,794	10,003
Previously rescheduled	3,111	5,612	8,723
Consolidated	8,161	7,637	15,798
Not previously rescheduled	6,115	3,505	9,620
Previously rescheduled	2,046	4,132	6,178
Amount to be paid[2]	12.4	18.8	15.6
Not previously rescheduled[2]	1.5	7.6	3.8
Previously rescheduled[2]	34.2	26.4	29.2
Moratorium interest	—	1,269	1,269
Post-cutoff date debt	1,272	2,905	4,177
Total debt service to be paid after consolidation[3]	2,431	5,943	8,374
On pre-cutoff date debt	(1,159)	(3,038)	(4,197)
Stock as of start of consolidation	56,981	—	56,981
Pre-cutoff date debt	44,043	—	44,043
Previously rescheduled	27,776	—	27,776
Post-cutoff date debt	12,938	—	12,938

Source: Agreed Minutes of debt reschedulings.

[1]Includes the reschedulings for Cameroon, Côte d'Ivoire, Dominican Republic, Ecuador, Guatemala, Jamaica (2), Jordan, Morocco, Nigeria, Peru (2), and the Philippines.

[2]Amount to be paid as percent of amount due.

[3]These figures exclude Peru's arrears on post-cutoff date debt of $761 million and moratorium payments of $447 million, which were deferred in 1991 beyond the consolidation period. The figures also exclude $320 million of moratorium interest deferred in 1991 and again in 1993, as well as $37 million of moratorium interest from the 1993 rescheduling that was deferred.

period (Table 10). Creditors also concluded comprehensive debt reductions and reorganizations with Poland and Egypt in April and May of 1991 (Box 3).

Other Middle-Income Countries

Standard terms continue to be applied for middle-income countries in the upper income range or where official bilateral creditors account for a small portion of the total debt. These terms have been applied to five countries since 1991. For these cases, Paris Club creditors consolidated nearly all of $7.9 billion due on original maturities but coverage of previously rescheduled debt was more limited ($8.2 billion of about $13.7 billion due). Taking into account moratorium interest of $1.6 billion, total actual debt-service payments on pre-cutoff date debt were reduced from $22.4 billion due to $7.9 billion (Table 11).

Official bilateral creditors meeting as the "Group of Official Creditors of the Former U.S.S.R." concluded a rescheduling agreement with the Russian Federation in early April 1993. As part of the agreement, Russia accepted full responsibility for the foreign debts of the former Soviet Union. The rescheduling covered arrears and debt-service obligations falling due during 1993 of about $15 billion.

Recent Experience with Debt Restructurings Involving Official Bilateral Creditors Not Participating in the Paris Club

Countries that request reschedulings from Paris Club creditors in support of their arrangements with the IMF typically also have debt-service obligations to official bilateral creditors that do not participate in Paris Club reschedulings. Paris Club creditors require as a condition for reschedulings that debtor countries seek debt relief on comparable terms from other creditors.[19] The IMF also has an interest in promoting agreements on these obligations because of its role in ensuring that relations between debtor countries and their creditors are conducted in an orderly manner and because the financing of IMF-supported programs usually requires appropriate relief on their obligations from all official bilateral creditors. The major official bilateral creditors that have not generally participated in the Paris Club include some Middle Eastern countries, some countries in the Western Hemisphere, and certain previously centrally planned economies (Eastern Europe, the former Soviet Union, and China).

This section first describes the policy of the Paris Club regarding comparability of treatment and then summarizes some of the agreements that have been reached between debtor countries and creditors outside the framework of the Paris Club. The experience of the last several years suggests that in most cases, where nonparticipating creditors have provided debt reschedulings on a bilateral basis, the agreements reached have been broadly in line with the terms granted by the Paris Club. The wide variations in the terms of the agreements, however, make direct comparisons with the terms applied by Paris Club creditors difficult. Moreover, agreements have not been reached in all cases.

Comparability of Treatment

A major objective of debt-rescheduling operations in the multilateral framework of the Paris Club has been to assure equitable burden sharing among different groups of creditors and between individual creditors. The Paris Club attaches great importance to the principle that all creditors should bear their part of the burden of financial support for a debtor country. Creditors that do not participate in reschedulings should not benefit unfairly from relief offered by participating creditors. For this reason, all Paris Club agreements contain clauses under which the debtor country agrees to seek terms comparable with those obtained in the Paris Club rescheduling from other creditors, including private creditors and suppliers. The provisions for debt relief from other official bilateral creditors are set out in a specific "most favored nation clause," which requires the debtor not to extend more favorable treatment to nonparticipating creditor countries

---

> **Box 3. Paris Club Debt Restructurings for Egypt and Poland**
>
> In early 1991, Paris Club creditors concluded comprehensive debt restructuring agreements with Egypt and Poland. These agreements, considered exceptional, had four important features.
>
> First, in contrast to previous Paris Club practice, the agreements covered the total stock of pre-cutoff date debt rather than consolidating debt service falling due over a limited period. In both cases, the debt restructuring covered about $30 billion.
>
> Second, the agreements provided for a debt reduction of 50 percent (in net present value terms). Creditors could choose among three equivalent options: an outright cancellation of debt by 50 percent, a reduction of interest rates, and a lesser interest rate reduction combined with a partial capitalization of moratorium interest at longer maturities (but no interest on capitalized moratorium interest).
>
> Third, the implementation of the debt reduction was staged over three years. Some reduction became effective at the outset, with the remainder to take place at specified intervals provided certain conditions were met regarding the debtors' implementation of IMF-supported adjustment programs. For Poland, creditors agreed to an immediate reduction of 30 percent to be followed by an additional 20 percent reduction after three years. For Egypt, creditors agreed to three stages: an immediate debt reduction of 15 percent, to be followed by an additional debt reduction of 15 percent in the second stage, and a final reduction of 20 percent. The agreements are subject to cancellation if conditions regarding the requirements of comparability of treatment of other creditors are not substantially fulfilled.
>
> Fourth, the repayment schedules were specifically tailored to the circumstances of the two countries, taking into account both immediate cash-flow requirements and repayment capacity over the medium term. For the first three years, repayments were fixed at a constant percentage of scheduled interest payments on the (pre-reduction) stock of debt: 20 percent for Poland and 70 percent for Egypt, reflecting the latter's higher initial payments capacity. Over the medium term, however, Egypt was granted a longer repayment schedule, with gradually rising payments over 25 years and over 35 years for concessional debt. The maturity for Poland was 18 years, with payments steeply rising toward the end of the period.

than that accorded to Paris Club creditors. The general policy applies to all creditors to which the rescheduling country has significant debt-service obligations with the notable exception of multilateral institutions, whose preferential status has long been accepted by official bilateral creditors.

In assessing whether action taken by nonparticipating creditors is comparable, Paris Club creditors are concerned not with the form that the debt restructuring takes, but rather with the effective

---

[19]Paris Club negotiations are open to all governments that have extended credits to the debtor country and that are prepared to accept the policies and procedures of the Club. The regular participants tend to be creditors from industrial countries, though a number of developing country creditors have participated in recent reschedulings.

Table 11. Other Middle-Income Rescheduling Countries: Amounts Due and Consolidated, 1991–June 1993[1]

(In millions of U.S. dollars)

	Arrears as of Start of Consolidation	Debt Service Falling Due During Consoli- dation Period	Total
Pre-cutoff date debt			
Debt service due	11,259[2]	11,132	22,391[2]
Not previously rescheduled	3,537	4,364	7,901
Previously rescheduled	6,972	6,768	13,740
Consolidated	7,524	8,564	16,088
Not previously rescheduled	3,500	4,364	7,864
Previously rescheduled	4,023	4,200	8,223
Amount to be paid[3]	33.2	23.1	28.1
Not previously rescheduled[3]	1.0	—	0.5
Previously rescheduled[3]	42.3	37.9	40.2
Moratorium interest	—	1,602	1,602
Post-cutoff date debt	296	2,426	2,722
Total debt service to be paid after consolidation	4,031	6,596	10,627
Pre-cutoff date debt	(3,735)	(4,170)	(7,905)
Stock as of start of consolidation	52,110	—	52,110
Pre-cutoff date debt	45,080	—	45,080
Previously rescheduled	28,169	—	28,169
Post-cutoff date debt	7,030	—	7,030

Source: Agreed Minutes of debt reschedulings.

[1]Includes the two reschedulings each for Argentina, Bulgaria (1991 and 1992), and Costa Rica (1991 and 1993), as well as for Brazil and Gabon.

[2]Includes $750 million of late interest not consolidated for Brazil.

[3]Amount to be paid as percent of amount due.

relief provided in cash-flow terms.[20] Also, in keeping with the underlying concern that all creditors should participate in financial support for the debtor country, Paris Club creditors have generally made some allowance in assessing comparability for continuing financial contributions by nonparticipating creditors. There is no presumption that the cutoff date established in the Paris Club Agreed Minute should apply to nonparticipating official bilateral creditors, but Paris Club creditors have generally accepted the exclusion from the comparability provisions of debt-service obligations arising from new credits if a specific cutoff date has been agreed between the debtor and the nonparticipating creditor and if the creditor continues to provide direct financial assistance to the debtor country concerned.

---

[20]Paris Club creditors have recognized the diverse institutional constraints faced by other official bilateral creditors and that both rescheduling and refinancing operations can be used to provide comparable debt relief. However, Paris Club creditors have emphasized that refinancing loans must provide untied cash relief over the relevant consolidation period. Thus, disbursements from tied project financing or linked directly to imports do not qualify as refinancing loans for comparability purposes.

Approaches Taken by Nonparticipating Official Bilateral Creditors

Creditors that have not participated in Paris Club reschedulings have adopted a wide variety of approaches in bilateral agreements with debtor countries. In some cases, creditors have provided new financing to meet their obligations in a manner consistent with the Paris Club requirements of comparability. In most cases, however, creditors have negotiated rescheduling agreements. Reflecting the absence of an established institutional forum for negotiations, individual creditor countries have developed different approaches, which have then been adapted to the individual circumstances of debtors. Some approaches have been innovative and have resulted in agreements on terms that go beyond those agreed by the Paris Club, including substantial concessions and stock-of-debt reductions to low-income countries. Table A11 provides a listing of some recent bilateral debt-restructuring agreements concluded in parallel with Paris Club agreements.[21]

---

[21]In many cases, obligations due to official bilateral creditors that do not participate in Paris Club reschedulings are small,

Latin American Creditors

Recent bilateral debt-restructuring agreements concluded by Latin American creditor countries in parallel with Paris Club agreements contained innovative features. Several creditors have explicitly provided for debt exchanges at a discount. In some cases, debtors were offered the option of buying the creditors' debt to commercial banks at a discount on the secondary market and then exchanging it for official debt of an equivalent face value owed to the creditor. This approach was used by Mexico in the case of Costa Rica in 1988, and has since been used extensively by Brazil, notably in the cases of Bolivia, Costa Rica, and Guyana.

Latin American creditor countries have generally agreed to reschedule most credits to other Latin American countries that are not channeled through and serviced by multilateral payments mechanisms. For example, in addition to the rescheduling agreed between Mexico and Costa Rica described above, Mexico and Venezuela both rescheduled on non-concessional terms debts owed by Costa Rica in 1991 and by Honduras in 1992 and 1993, respectively. Venezuela has rescheduled on nonconcessional terms debts owed by Jamaica, in the period 1990–92, and by Guyana, in 1991.

Some creditors have also applied more innovative arrangements for low-income countries. For example, in 1989, Argentina and Bolivia reached agreement on the mutual cancellation of Bolivian debt to Argentina and Argentinean debt to Bolivia. This resulted in the effective forgiveness of 72 percent of Bolivia's debt in 1992. Mexico and Venezuela agreed to a buy-back of debt owed by the Dominican Republic at a discount of 68 percent. A similar agreement was concluded between Brazil and the Dominican Republic in 1993. Guyana was able to secure, in 1989, reschedulings on concessional terms of debt owed to Trinidad and Tobago and to Barbados and other members of the Caribbean Multilateral Clearing Facility.

Finally, in the case of Nicaragua several Latin American creditors agreed to substantial debt cancellation. Under agreements reached in 1991, Columbia, Mexico, and Venezuela reached agreements that provided for debt cancellation equivalent to about 95 percent of the debt in net present value terms. Under the agreements with Mexico and Venezuela, repayment of debts will be made in 40 years, with the full face value of principal obligations being secured through a zero coupon bond. Payment of interest charges begins only in the seventh year, provided that Nicaragua's exports have increased substantially. Resources to purchase the zero coupon bonds were obtained from the reactivation of partial financing of oil purchases from Mexico and Venezuela. A similar agreement is currently under discussion with Argentina.

Arab Creditors

Most of the outstanding loans made by Arab creditors are to countries in North Africa and sub-Saharan Africa. Arab creditors have generally been responsive to requests from these countries for reschedulings, and have on occasion agreed to reschedulings on concessional terms and to debt cancellations. For example, in 1990, Saudi Arabia canceled some $5.7 billion of debt owed by countries affected by the Gulf War, including $2.8 billion owed by Morocco and $2.3 billion owed by Egypt. Kuwait canceled $1.9 billion owed by Egypt, United Arab Emirates canceled $304 million owed by Egypt, and Qatar canceled $93 million owed by Egypt at this time. Moreover, Saudi Arabia also canceled in 1991 some $300 million in official credits owed by low-income countries in sub-Saharan Africa. More recently, Saudi Arabia and Kuwait have concluded individual reschedulings with some low-income African countries, including Burkina Faso, Mauritania, and Mali.

China

In recent years, China has agreed to reschedulings on highly concessional terms for a number of debtor countries, including conversion of payments into local currency. For example, the Chinese Government has agreed to a moratorium on debt-service payments from Mali, has repeatedly rescheduled loans to Guyana and Benin interest free, and has provided interest-free reschedulings for other countries.

Former Soviet Union

Progress on the very substantial outstanding debts owed by a number of rescheduling countries to the former Soviet Union has been slower as the uncertainties resulting from the transition in the former Soviet Union led to considerable delays in the initiation of discussions.[22] While the Russian Federation (which has assumed the claims of the coun-

---

and the coverage in this table is not exhaustive. However, it does cover most of the major agreements that have been reached since 1987.

[22]Available information on discussions between other former countries of the Council of Mutual Economic Assistance (CMEA) and their rescheduling country debtors is limited, but it appears that difficulties and delays have also been experienced in these cases, and that few agreements have been concluded with other former CMEA countries. Where such agreements have been reached they have often been based on debt-conversion schemes.

tries of the former Soviet Union) has now begun discussions with most of the countries concerned and has concluded a number of agreements, in many cases discussions are still at a preliminary stage. Moreover, agreements on debts owed to the countries of the former Soviet Union have been made more complex by unresolved issues of data verification and reconciliation as well as the fact that most of these debts are denominated in rubles but are subject to conversion at an exchange rate linked to a basket of currencies. This implies an exchange rate very different from the current market rate.

Reflecting these difficulties, only a few agreements have been finalized between the Russian Federation and rescheduling countries. Under a comprehensive agreement reached with Jordan in 1992, Jordan bought back at a discount (in cash and kind) debt from the Russian Federation with a face value of $614 million.[23]

In other cases, the Russian Federation has agreed to the continuation of rescheduling agreements reached between debtor countries and the countries of the former Soviet Union. For example, for Afghanistan, Mongolia, Mali, and the Lao People's Democratic Republic, the Russian Federation has continued agreements for reduction or deferral of scheduled payments originally negotiated between the countries concerned and the former U.S.S.R.. In some cases, these agreements have implied substantial debt relief. For example, for Mali, the Russian Federation accepted a complete moratorium on debt-service payments made in 1992 and very limited payments in local currency to cover payments falling due in 1993. Negotiations are under way with other rescheduling countries that have substantial debts to the countries of the former Soviet Union, including Benin, Ethiopia, Mozambique, and Nicaragua.

Official Bilateral Debt Forgiveness Initiatives

This subsection reviews recent experience with official bilateral debt forgiveness initiatives. Over the past decade, there have been two distinct rounds of actions in this area. First, in response to the 1978 resolution of the United Nations Conference on Trade and Development (UNCTAD), a number of creditors canceled ODA debts of the least-developed countries and provided all new ODA to these

---

[23]The Russian Federation has also concluded a comprehensive rescheduling agreement with India, with part of India's debt to the former Soviet Union being rescheduled on nonconcessional terms, and part of it being rescheduled on highly concessional terms, involving an even stream of payments over 45 years.

countries in the form of grants. Some $3 billion was canceled under this initiative through 1988. Over two thirds of the total amount was owed by developing countries in sub-Saharan Africa. Donor countries acting in response to the resolution included Canada, Denmark, Finland, France, Germany, the Netherlands, Sweden, Switzerland, and the United Kingdom.

During 1985–91, the most recent years for which data are available on a consistent basis, the total amount of debt cancellations by official bilateral creditors totaled $26.0 billion (Table A12). These debt cancellations have all been implemented on a purely bilateral basis in contrast to the multilateral reschedulings by Paris Club creditors. Countries benefiting from these initiatives have included both rescheduling countries and those that have avoided debt-servicing difficulties.

Debt Forgiveness Initiatives in 1989–90

A second round of debt forgiveness, focused on heavily indebted countries, started in 1989. In contrast to the first round, the more recent cancellations have typically been linked to debtor country policy performance. They covered mostly ODA credits extended in the more recent past, and in some cases other loans made or guaranteed by creditor governments; eligibility for debt forgiveness was broadened to other low-income and some middle-income countries; debt conversion mechanisms were often included. Countries benefiting from these initiatives have included both rescheduling countries and countries that have avoided debt-servicing difficulties. Many of the initiatives were directed at heavily indebted low-income sub-Saharan African countries:

• In May 1989, the Government of *France* announced that it would cancel ODA debts owed by 35 low-income African countries. The initiative covered debts contracted before the end of 1988 with a face value of $3.1 billion.

• In 1988–89, the Government of *Germany* undertook cancellation of ODA credits with a face value of some $1.4 billion. This initiative covered loans to least-developed countries and other low-income African countries and also included arrears that had not been covered in the previous initiatives.

• In July 1989, the Government of the *United States* announced its intention to forgive some $500 million of ODA loans to certain low-income African countries, and to provide future ODA to these countries on a grant basis. The cancellations were to be tranched and conditioned on implementation of structural adjustment programs supported by the IMF and the World Bank.

• In July 1989, the Government of *Belgium*

announced forgiveness of some $330 million of bilateral official and officially guaranteed credits to several African countries.

• In the second half of 1989, the Government of *Canada* canceled some $570 million of ODA loans to 13 sub-Saharan African countries, while continuing the policy of providing ODA on a grant basis only.

There were also initiatives in 1990 for countries outside of sub-Saharan Africa including the following:

• In March 1990, the Government of *Canada* announced its intention to seek the cancellation of some $150 million of ODA credits that had been extended to 11 countries in the Caribbean region.

• In November 1990, the Government of *Germany* agreed to cancel about $500 million of ODA credits to Poland and to convert a further $350 million into domestic currency funds to finance investment projects.

• In the second half of 1990, the Government of the *United States* canceled some $6.6 billion of credits that had originally been extended on commercial terms to Egypt under certain bilateral assistance programs, some of which were in arrears. Prior to cancellation, the terms on these credits had been adjusted to those on ODA credits.

More Recent Initiatives

Several creditor countries have recently announced further debt-reduction initiatives that involve various forms of debt conversions, cancellations or buybacks. Four initiatives by the governments of the United States, Canada, Switzerland, and France are described below. In all cases, the implementation of the initiatives is linked to appropriate policy performance by debtor countries.

The *U.S. Enterprise for the Americas Initiative (EAI)*, announced in June 1990, aims to enhance development prospects through action in the areas of trade, investment, and debt. Under the EAI, debts owed by developing countries in the Western Hemisphere to the U.S. Government can be reduced provided that the country (1) is undertaking macroeconomic and structural reforms; (2) is liberalizing its investment regime; and (3) has concluded a debt-restructuring agreement with its commercial bank creditors.

The initiative provides for a reduction of concessional debts, including loans disbursed under programs of food assistance (Public Law 480) and development assistance (Agency for International Development (AID)). Countries benefiting from debt reductions may make interest payments on the remaining debt in local currency if they negotiate "Framework Agreements" under which these

resources would be committed to environmental or child development projects. The remaining principal is to be repaid in U.S. dollars. In addition, some part of the nonconcessional debt owed to U.S. Eximbank and the Commodity Credit Corporation may either be bought back by the debtor or used to facilitate debt-for-equity, debt-for-nature, or debt-for-development swaps.

Under the EAI, the United States has reduced about $875 million of the bilateral foreign assistance and food assistance obligations of Argentina, Bolivia, Chile, Colombia, El Salvador, Jamaica, and Uruguay. If bilateral framework agreements have been negotiated, $154 million in local currency resources could be channeled to environmental and child survival projects in these countries. The U.S. Congress has authorized the reduction of AID debt, and swaps of nonconcessional loans; and appropriations have been obtained for a further $90 million for EAI debt reduction in fiscal year 1993.

At the 1992 "Earth Summit" in Rio de Janeiro, the Canadian Government proposed its *Debt Conversion Initiative for Sustainable Development*. Under this initiative up to $145 million of ODA loans owed by developing countries in the Western Hemisphere can be converted into local currency funds to help finance environmental and other sustainable development projects. Countries eligible for debt relief under this initiative include Brazil, Colombia, Costa Rica, Cuba, Dominican Republic, El Salvador, Guatemala, and Peru. Debt conversions will be negotiated and implemented on a case-by-case basis. They will be subject to specific conditions related in particular to the promotion of human rights and democratic principles, as well as to economic policies. The schedule of payments in local currency is to be determined on the basis of a country's capacity to pay and of the financing requirements of the projects being supported. Provision will also be made to safeguard scheduled payments against erosion of their real value.

The *Swiss Debt Reduction Facility* became operational in January 1991, with an original endowment of Sfr 100 million, which was later expanded to Sfr 500 million. The facility can be used for debt relief measures over a period of five to seven years. It is estimated that the facility will help eliminate debts of around $1.8 billion. The aim of the facility is to support highly indebted low-income countries that have established strong reform records, provided they (1) have acceptable conditions of governance; (2) have adequate debt-management systems; and (3) implement programs supported by multilateral financial institutions. The 45 countries eligible for debt relief under this facility include the least-developed countries and other developing countries that either obtain Paris Club reschedulings on enhanced concessional terms or are recipients of Swiss ODA that has been rescheduled under the Paris Club framework.

The resources of the facility can be used for a wide range of measures, including buy-backs of officially insured Swiss export credits and commercial noninsured debt, contributions to the clearing of arrears, and the financing of payments to the multilaterals. Alternatively, debt cancellation can be linked to the creation by the debtor government of a local currency counterpart fund that would be used to finance development projects.

In March 1992, the facility contributed $42 million to a buy-back from Swiss exporters (95 percent participated) of the noninsured portion of officially supported claims on 22 mostly African countries; this retired debt of a face value of $0.2 billion. The total value of debt eliminated under this operation, including the portion guaranteed by the Swiss export credit agency that will be written off as it falls due, is estimated at $1 billion.

The French Government announced a new debt initiative at the 1992 Franco-African Summit held in Libreville (Gabon), known as the *Libreville Debt Initiative*, under which France would cancel or convert ODA debts through a debt conversion fund of FF 4 billion set up at the end of 1992. The initiative applies to Cameroon, the Congo, Côte d'Ivoire, and Gabon. The cancellations would occur as counterparts to the development projects included in the government investment programs and approved by the Caisse Française de Developpement (CFD). These projects can be in the areas of environmental protection, social and educational development, productivity improvements, and agricultural development. Individual investment projects eligible under the initiative may reach up to FF 100 million.

Debt Conversions Under Paris Club Agreements

In September 1990, Paris Club creditors introduced in debt-rescheduling agreements for lower middle-income countries a provision for debt conversions on a voluntary basis in the form of debt-for-equity, debt-for-aid, debt-for-nature, and other debt-for-local currency operations. The amount of debt that could be converted under this provision was limited to the greater of $10 million or 10 percent of consolidated commercial credits; however, 100 percent of ODA and direct government loans could be included. The provision was subsequently included in the new menu of enhanced concessions.

To date, debt-conversion agreements have been concluded by France and the United Kingdom. The agreement between France and Egypt, concluded in March 1993, provides for a conversion of bilateral claims into investments. The conversions are to take place in several tranches, each of which will be subject to competitive bidding from investors. In the projects approved by the authorities in the first tranche, claims worth FF 550 million were auctioned. The Export Credit Guarantee Department (ECGD) of the United Kingdom has concluded debt conversions with Egypt, Nigeria, and Tanzania, mostly for developmental, health, and education projects.

While debt-conversion agreements are a potentially useful option for debtors and creditors, experience has shown the need for caution in approaching such schemes. Unless financed through privatization proceeds, conversion schemes typically imply the creation of domestic debt that can be costly to service or is monetized, and thus can undermine macroeconomic stabilization. Moreover, once all the features of the scheme are fully taken into account, such schemes may involve the provision of a substantial implicit subsidy to the investor. Finally, even with a large subsidy, the true additionality of the new investment may be dubious. Governments need to be careful to ensure that such schemes do not undermine macroeconomic policies, are transparent, and avoid excessive subsidization.

IV

Recent Developments in New Financing from Official Bilateral Sources

Official bilateral creditors and donors are by far the most important source of financing for most developing countries. Recent developments are marked by three broad trends. First, aggregate gross disbursements increased rapidly by an average of about 11 percent a year between 1986 and 1991. Second, much of this increase took the form of ODA flows to low-income countries: bilateral ODA was the most important source of direct external financial assistance for most low-income countries. Third, new flows to both low- and middle-income countries were increasingly linked to the implementation of appropriate economic policies. Countries that pursued adjustment and reform programs and maintained orderly relations with creditors, including through reschedulings, continued to obtain large amounts of external financial support. Resources were less readily available to countries with mixed records of policy implementation.

Instruments

Official creditors provide financial support to developing countries through a wide range of instruments. Bilateral financial assistance has taken the form of direct financing (grants and new credits, often on concessional terms) as well as indirect support in the form of insurance cover and other guarantees extended by official export credit agencies for private sector loans. Bilateral creditors and donors also provide capital contributions to multilateral institutions, guarantee these institutions' borrowing on capital markets, and have provided cofinancing in conjunction with disbursements by multilateral institutions. Finally, as described in Section III, bilateral creditors have provided cash-flow relief in support of countries' adjustment programs.

This wide variety of instruments and channels for official financial support has allowed official creditors to tailor the scope and terms of external financial assistance closely to developing countries' circumstances and to move promptly in support of countries' macroeconomic and structural adjustment programs. Official assistance is frequently coordinated by Consultative Groups. Such groups have traditionally met to arrange financing for low-income countries, but in the recent past similar mechanisms have been used to coordinate financial assistance to economies in transition in Central and Eastern Europe and in the countries of the former Soviet Union.

There are important conceptual and coverage differences between the creditor-based (OECD) and debtor-based (World Bank) data sources for official bilateral finance (Box 4). Neither source provides a comprehensive coverage of official resource flows to developing countries. The OECD system excludes some creditors, while the World Bank system excludes certain flows. As a consequence, no single picture of official bilateral flows to developing countries exists. This section draws largely on data compiled by the OECD and the World Bank. For the section on Officially Supported Export Credits, unpublished data compiled by the Export Credit Group of the OECD and the Berne Union have been used.

Recent Developments

Total *net* bilateral disbursements by Development Assistance Committee (DAC) member countries (the OECD system) are estimated to have increased in 1992 to $47 billion, from $46 billion in the previous year, and again accounted for about two thirds of ODA flows from all sources, including multilateral institutions (Table 12). Bilateral ODA remained broadly constant at $41 billion during 1992 (87 percent of total official bilateral financing to developing countries—the same percentage as in 1985). The share of bilateral ODA channeled to low-income countries, however, continued to increase, and reached 60 percent in 1992, compared with 52 percent in 1989 and 45 percent in 1985 (Table 13).

In 1991, total *gross* bilateral disbursements to all developing countries increased by 8.5 percent to around $85 billion (Tables A13 and A14),[24] while

---

[24]These statistics do not capture large gross disbursements to countries in Central and Eastern Europe, which continue to receive substantial assistance from the DAC member countries, including on concessional terms. The DAC Secretariat has been recently asked to begin collecting and publishing data on finan-

Box 4. Data Sources for Official Bilateral Financing Flows

The variety of instruments used by official bilateral creditors makes a comprehensive analysis of bilateral financial flows a complex undertaking. Caution is also called for in interpreting the data because of systemic differences in the collection of statistics. World Bank data are derived from debtor-based information systems and are published annually in *World Debt Tables*; military debt is excluded. Data from the Organization for Economic Cooperation and Development (OECD) include comprehensive statistics on gross and net disbursements published in the *Geographic Distribution of Financial Flows to Developing Countries*. Preliminary estimates of aggregate net disbursements are released in press communiqués for the Report of the Chairman of the Development Assistance Committee of the OECD (DAC). The comprehensive individual country data for 1991 became available only in late 1992, while the preliminary aggregate estimates for 1992 were released in June 1993. Country groups used in the OECD reports are different from standard country classifications used in the IMF. For OECD country listings, see Table A8.

For officially supported *export credits*, debtor reporting systems classify disbursements from officially insured credits as disbursements from banks or suppliers. The OECD creditor reporting system provides data on creditors' exposure, including contingent liabilities under insurance contracts, but data are generally available only with a considerable time lag. More recent data are available on a commitment basis to a number of debtor countries; these data typically include all future interest payments. Data on officially supported export credits are published in *Statistics on External Indebtedness: Bank and Trade Related Non-Bank External Claims on Individual Borrowing Countries and Territories* prepared jointly by the Bank for International Settlements (BIS) and the OECD.

total flows have remained broadly unchanged at $8.5 billion, but total grants increased by 9 percent to reach $7.5 billion while disbursements of ODA loans contracted by 39 percent to less than $1 billion (Table A13). For other low-income countries, a sharp increase in total official flows, from $27 billion in 1990 to $31 billion in 1991, reflected a near doubling in ODA loan disbursements to $12 billion, mostly accounted for by loan disbursements from the United States and Japan to Egypt.

Official bilateral flows to the *lower middle-income countries*, increased by some 5 percent (Table A13). Here, too, the composition shifted toward grants and ODA loans, which together increased by 17 percent to $7.5 billion. In contrast, reported flows to upper middle-income countries recorded a sharp fall in non-ODA official loans. Official bilateral flows to all middle-income countries declined by 2 percent in 1991 to $33 billion, partially reversing the upward trend of recent years. Official bilateral financing of middle-income (and especially upper middle-income countries) continued to include large flows of officially supported export credits, and disbursements under cofinancing arrangements with multilateral institutions (discussed below).

There were also marked changes in the geographical distribution of gross official bilateral flows in 1991 (Table A14). The decline in total financing to sub-Saharan Africa, for example, reflected in large part the impact of uneven policy implementation as evidenced by the emergence of arrears, particularly in Cameroon, Côte d'Ivoire, and Kenya. The sharp increase in disbursements to North Africa and the Middle East reflected exceptional disbursements of concessional financing to countries affected by the Gulf crisis.

Official Bilateral Financing to Rescheduling Countries

Official bilateral creditors have continued to provide extensive new disbursements to countries that required debt reschedulings. A crucial factor in enabling financial support to continue despite debt-servicing difficulties has been the maintenance of fixed cutoff dates in Paris Club rescheduling agreements. Gross flows to all rescheduling countries reached $39 billion in 1991, an increase of 22 percent since 1989 (Table 14). While the figures for 1991 may overstate the underlying level on account of the exceptional flows in connection with the Gulf crisis, over the period 1989–91, official bilateral flows were equivalent to about 44 percent of these countries' own foreign exchange earnings from exports and were almost three times as large as disbursements by multilaterals.

ODA flows increased by over 23 percent, to $54 billion. Both ODA loans and grants recorded strong growth while other official bilateral credits and loans declined for a second consecutive year.

Recent years witnessed important changes in the composition of official bilateral flows. For the *low-income countries*, concessional debt restructuring and ODA debt cancellations accompanied a continued increase in the concessionality of new financial flows as official bilateral creditors shifted new flows further toward pure grant financing and away from debt-creating flows. This was particularly evident for the least-developed countries. For this group,

---

cial flows to these countries. The data on *gross* and *net* disbursements are not strictly comparable: net disbursements exclude officially supported export credits, while these are included in gross disbursements.

Table 12. Official Financing Flows to Developing Countries, 1985–92[1]

	1985	1990	1991	1992[2]	1985	1990	1991	1992[2]
	(In billions of U.S. dollars)				*(In percent of total)*			
Total official flows net	44.4	69.4	70.1	72.3	100.0	100.0	100.0	100.0
By category								
Bilateral	28.6	46.0	46.2	47.3	64.4	66.3	66.0	65.4
Official development assistance (ODA)[3]	24.8	39.2	41.3	41.3	55.9	56.5	59.0	57.1
Other	3.8	6.8	4.9	6.0	8.3	9.7	7.0	8.3
Multilateral	15.8	23.4	23.9	25.0	35.1	33.7	34.0	34.6
ODA[3]	8.1	13.2	16.1	17.0	18.2	19.2	23.0	23.5
Other	7.1	10.2	7.8	8.0	16.0	14.7	11.0	11.1
By income group[4]								
Low-income	20.5	37.5	40.3	42.2	46.2	54.0	57.6	58.4
Middle-income	17.5	24.7	21.3	22.1	39.4	35.6	30.4	30.6
Memorandum items								
Total net flows[5]	78.2	130.5	134.0	175.6	. . .	. . .	. . .	. . .
Official in percent of total	56.8	53.2	52.2	41.2	. . .	. . .	. . .	. . .
Bilateral ODA as percent of bilateral	86.7	85.2	89.4	87.3	. . .	. . .	. . .	. . .
Multilateral ODA as percent of multilateral	51.3	56.4	67.3	68.0	. . .	. . .	. . .	. . .

Source: Organization for Economic Cooperation and Development (OECD).

[1]Official development finance including grants and bilateral and multilateral loans, and excluding export credits.

[2]Preliminary.

[3]Excluding debt forgiveness of non-ODA claims in 1990–92.

[4]OECD income group classification. Unallocated amounts (mostly ODA) account for the difference between the sum of the components and the total.

[5]Including official development finance, export credits, foreign direct investment, international bank and bond lending, grants by nongovernmental organizations, and other private flows.

Table 13. Distribution of Net ODA Disbursements to Developing Countries by Income Group, 1985–92

	1985	1986	1987	1988	1989	1990	1991	1992[1]
Total net official development assistance (ODA)[2] *(in millions of U.S. dollars)*	32.9	39.1	43.8	47.5	48.6	52.6	57.4	58.3
Of which share *(in percent)*[3]								
Middle-income countries	30.1	27.9	26.7	23.6	23.5	27.8	24.9	24.5
Low-income countries	52.0	54.2	53.4	57.1	56.8	61.4	60.1	63.0
Bilateral net ODA *(in millions of U.S. dollars)*	24.8	29.8	33.8	36.4	36.3	39.2	41.3	41.3
Of which share *(in percent)*[3]								
Middle-income countries	36.3	32.9	31.4	27.2	26.9	33.2	29.5	29.1
Low-income countries	45.2	47.3	46.1	50.8	51.8	56.9	56.9	59.8
Memorandum item								
Share of multilateral in total net ODA	24.6	23.8	22.8	23.2	25.2	25.5	28.0	29.2

Sources: OECD; and IMF staff estimates.

[1]Preliminary estimate.

[2]Excludes intra-developing country reserve flows.

[3]The residual includes unallocated amounts that exist when geographical distribution of flows is unavailable or not possible, for example, in the case of foreign-financed regional projects, scholarships in the donor country, etc. These amounts declined as a proportion of total net disbursements from 18 percent in 1985 to 13 percent in 1992.

Table 14. Official Financing Flows to Low-Income Rescheduling Countries, 1989–91

	Total Official Bilateral Flows[1]			Share of ODA Total Bilateral Official[2]			Bilateral ODA Flows	*Memorandum* Multilateral Disbursements[3]
	1989	1990	1991	1989	1990	1991	1989–91	1989–91
	(In millions of U.S. dollars)			*(In percent)*			*(In percent of exports)[4]*	
Total low-income	**8,056**	**10,450**	**10,992**	**76**	**88**	**92**	**70**	**23**
Angola	224	235	131	40	66	92	3	1
Benin	234	151	171	67	87	100	43	21
Bolivia	382	371	828	84	98	94	50	24
Burkina Faso	229	270	284	91	92	99	79	32
Central African Republic	103	109	118	100	94	86	48	32
Chad	128	180	138	100	100	100	67	30
Equatorial Guinea	26	20	14	74	100	100	51	18
Ethiopia	458	561	485	87	91	94	71	21
Gambia, The	211	67	56	28	87	100	35	13
Guinea	208	180	232	98	85	79	23	15
Guinea-Bissau	73	65	48	72	95	99	155	84
Guyana	36	142	219	80	45	71	30	27
Honduras	240	390	675	85	98	94	33	10
Liberia	—	160	71	. . .	27	78	9	. . .
Madagascar	250	446	422	83	95	86	68	28
Malawi	214	251	238	89	90	94	56	30
Mali	304	313	291	100	100	98	86	24
Mauritania	159	102	127	100	98	96	26	12
Mozambique	550	737	866	100	100	94	227	29
Nicaragua	191	269	926	96	100	100	140	15
Niger	224	271	314	98	99	88	70	14
Senegal	565	791	532	99	98	90	45	8
Sierra Leone	96	53	67	82	75	99	42	3
Somalia	335	259	116	86	100	100	242	42
Sudan	460	409	385	100	100	96	78	29
Tanzania	732	920	896	95	97	98	143	33
Togo	121	184	154	95	87	89	20	7
Uganda	215	283	295	75	90	99	101	74
Zaïre	612	1,419	1,020	75	50	60	30	11
Zambia	503	841	870	63	91	79	48	12
Memorandum item								
All rescheduling countries	31,992	34,578	39,158	62	75	80	44	15

Sources: OECD; World Bank Debtor Reporting System; and IMF staff estimates.
Note: ODA denotes official development assistance; DAC denotes Development Assistance Committee of the OECD.
[1]From DAC countries only, including grants, and gross disbursements of ODA loans, and official and officially guaranteed export credits. In 1990 and 1991 include large debt forgiveness and debt reorganization.
[2]Arithmetic average of individual country ratios.
[3]Excluding use of IMF credit.
[4]In percent of exports of goods and services. Arithmetic average of annual ratios in 1989–91.

Official bilateral flows to low-income rescheduling countries witnessed a particularly sharp increase averaging 17 percent a year over 1989–91, to reach $11 billion in 1991 (Table 14). The importance of these flows can be gauged by the fact that they were equivalent to 70 percent of these countries' export earnings over the period. Moreover, there was a pronounced shift toward more concessional financing as 92 percent of official bilateral flows qualified as ODA in 1992, compared with 76 percent two years earlier. A number of countries with IMF-supported adjustment programs experienced particularly marked increases in official bilateral flows between 1989 and 1991. During this period, these flows more than doubled for Bolivia, Guyana, Honduras, and Nicaragua and increased by more than 50 percent for Madagascar, Mozambique, and Zambia.

The combination of appropriate economic policies and increased availability of concessional financing has enabled several low-income rescheduling countries to make some progress toward external viability as noted in the recent review of experience under ESAF arrangements.[25] This progress is attributable to both concessional debt relief (cancellation of existing debts as well as concessional rescheduling) and to strong export growth. However, as underlined in Section II, progress has not been sufficient to enable these countries to graduate from the rescheduling process. In countries where program implementation was uneven and where export growth was adversely affected by external factors, the impact of concessional debt relief on scheduled interest payments was generally offset by the burden of new debt, including arrears. Furthermore, slippages in adjustment programs or project implementation tended to delay disbursements of aid, thereby leading to a hardening of average financing terms.

Officially Supported Export Credits

Following the onset of the debt crisis, there was a precipitous decline in export credit activity, and new export credit business remained low throughout the 1980s.[26] In 1989, however, lending activity to middle-income countries started to pick up again, and recent data indicate that this upswing has continued.[27] Data compiled by the Export Credit Group of the OECD suggest that the net flow of export credits to middle-income countries increased by 17 percent in 1991, although lending to low-income countries declined by about 2 percent. Preliminary data for 1992 confirm the continued growth in export credit activity. The main reason for this upturn was the volume of new credits extended to countries in Eastern and Central Europe.

The *Berne Union survey* on the commitments of export credit agencies to selected developing countries[28] shows that agencies' medium- and long-term exposure remained broadly unchanged during 1992, while short-term business expanded by over 60 percent. The data on the flow of new commitments

show that Berne Union agencies' new business is concentrated in middle-income countries that have either avoided, or successfully addressed, debt-servicing difficulties, including, for example, Argentina, the Czech Republic, Hungary, Mexico, the Philippines, and Venezuela. Countries with uneven policy records, particularly as regards payments arrears, have generally received only modest new commitments. The significant new commitments to low-income countries (particularly China, India, and Indonesia) reflect, in part, the commercial element of mixed (or "tied aid") credits (discussed below). Finally, the Berne Union data also record large new commitments to the Russian Federation.

The upswing in export credit activity that began in 1989 now seems to be well established, and while many middle-income countries are emerging from debt-servicing difficulties and are regaining access to capital markets, further increases in officially supported export credits appear likely. Export credit agencies' involvement could, however, be constrained by a number of factors. The demand for long-term financing for large-scale infrastructural projects will be limited by reductions in public sector investment budgets. The scale and composition of private sector investment has tended to require more modest external financing of somewhat shorter maturities. Moreover, export credit agencies have become more commercially oriented based on a more stringent evaluation and management of risk, a tendency that has been reinforced by the privatization of a number of agencies. Finally, agencies have generally taken the view that highly concessional flows are more appropriate for low-income countries than normal export credits.

Cofinancing

In recent years, official bilateral creditors (including export credit agencies) were the largest source of cofinancing with multilateral creditors. They provided over two thirds of cofinancing by the World Bank during its fiscal years 1992 and 1993. The largest share was provided by Japan;[29] substantial contributions were also made by the United States and several European countries.

In the fiscal years 1992 and 1993 together, the World Bank approved 234 projects for cofinancing with an average total value per year of $12 billion, compared with $9 billion in the 1991 fiscal year.[30]

[25]See, Susan Schadler and others, *Economic Adjustment in Low-Income Countries; Experience Under Enhanced Structural Adjustment Facility*, Occasional Paper, No. 106 (Washington: International Monetary Fund, September 1993).

[26]The interpretation of developments in officially supported export credits is hampered by the lack of reliable and timely data (Box 4).

[27]For more details on officially supported credits, see G. G. Johnson, Matthew Fisher, and Elliott Harris, *Officially Supported Export Credits: Developments and Prospects*, World Economic and Financial Surveys (Washington: International Monetary Fund, May 1990).

[28]In the Berne Union data, commitments of export credits include agencies' contingent liabilities in respect of principal (disbursed and not disbursed), as well as all covered interest. Country-by-country developments must be interpreted with caution as they are sensitive to the timing of individual large contracts. The flow of new commitments provides a leading indicator of actual disbursements.

[29]Japan has also provided cofinancing of Asian Development Bank (AsDB) and Inter-American Development Bank (IDB) operations, as well as parallel lending with the IMF.

[30]This includes both financing in parallel with adjustment operations, and financing of investment projects. The total cost of these projects was $72 billion, of which $24 billion was financed by the World Bank.

This reflected mostly a surge in 1992 in World Bank operations in sectors such as power and water, which attract cofinancing. The decline in such infrastructure projects, together with reductions in the aid budgets of several donors in the fiscal year 1993, led to a 15 percent fall in the total value of projects cofinanced with the World Bank.

The second largest source of cofinancing of World Bank operations was cofinancing by other multilaterals. During the World Bank's fiscal years 1992 and 1993, cofinancing by the Inter-American Development Bank (IDB) amounted to nearly $3 billion and accounted for 32 percent of cofinancing in this category. The recent increase in IDB cofinancing reflects the introduction of sector lending into its lending program. Cofinancing by the Asian Development Bank (AsDB) usually takes the form of parallel financing of separate projects within a sector rather than cofinancing of a single project. Cofinancing by the AsDB increased to around $400 million last year. Cofinancing by the African Development Bank (AfDB) of World Bank projects increased from $170 million in 1985 to $525 million in 1991 and focused on several key programs, such as women in development, private sector development, and regional economic cooperation. A new cofinancing program (Export Credit Loan Arrangement Technique) has recently been introduced by the European Bank for Reconstruction and Development (EBRD). This program offers several advantages to export credit agencies and seeks to streamline the complex procedures and negotiations entailed in more conventional cofinancing techniques. While private creditors' involvement in cofinancing has increased, it remains small.

Mixed Aid Finance

"Mixed credits" encompass all forms of commercial tied-aid credits that have a concessional element—as defined by the OECD Consensus on officially supported export credits (the "Consensus")—produced either by mixing grants and commercial loans or by direct subsidies on commercial loans. To limit the general subsidization of exports through export finance, export credit agencies have agreed to be bound by the provisions of the Consensus that established guidelines concerning financial terms and also set minimum concessional element requirements for mixed credits. These guidelines have gradually eliminated concessionality for richer countries and raised the minimum concessional element for poorer countries (see Box 5).

An important development was the agreement on February 15, 1992 among Consensus participants to

---

Box 5: Guidelines for Officially Supported Export Credits

The Arrangement on Guidelines for Officially Supported Export Credits, established in 1978, initially followed the Development Assistance Committee (DAC) criterion for determining the concessional element of mixed credits, using a concept of the grant element calculated at a flat 10 percent discount rate. This gave countries with low interest rate currencies a competitive advantage over countries with high interest rate currencies; as nominal interest rates were low, only small interest subsidies were required for loans to yield a high grant element. Similarly, for credits that mixed concessional and commercial loans, comparatively small portions of concessional assistance were needed to meet the required grant element. To redress this situation, the participants in the consensus decided in June 1986 to move in two steps (July 1987 and July 1988) to a formula for calculating the concessional element of aid credits, now to be called the "concessionality level." The formula gives 75 percent of the weight to a market-related rate and a 25 percent weight to the flat 10 percent discount rate, and thus more closely reflected market interest rates. In addition, the minimum concessionality level for Category III (low-income) countries was raised to 50 percent, and for Category II (middle-income) countries, to 30 percent on July 15,

1987 and to 35 percent a year later (except for ships and untied aid).

The new rules agreed on February 15, 1992 specify the following.
- For "better-off developing countries: Tied aid financing shall not be extended to countries whose per capita GNP makes them ineligible for 17 or 20 year loans from the World Bank."
- "Commercial viability: Tied and partially untied concessional or aid credits, except for credits to LLDCs (Least Developed Countries), shall not be extended to public and private projects that normally should be commercially viable if financed on market or Arrangement terms."
- The Participants also agreed to two key tests for evaluating whether projects are eligible for aid financing:
  (1) whether the project lacks capacity, with appropriate pricing determined on market principles, to generate cash flow sufficient to cover the project's operating costs and to service the capital employed, or
  (2) if it is reasonable to conclude, based on communication with other participants, that it is unlikely that the project can be financed on market or Arrangement terms.

amend the guidelines on tied-aid credits to "*better-off developing countries*." The new rules limit the use of tied aid for projects in those countries and thus reinforce the trend away from concessional financing for commercially attractive projects that could be financed by export credits and private financing. This move toward eliminating subsidies for private sector projects in middle-income countries should lead to a more careful evaluation of projects. It should also permit a shift in ODA resources and thus greater concessionality in lending to the poorest countries.

Over the past years, the minimum concessionality level on credits to the poorer countries allowed under the OECD Consensus has been increased in several steps and a large portion of aid credits is provided with a concessionality level just over the minimum level. The poorest developing countries continue to receive over half of all mixed credits, even though the share of these credits to the better-off developing countries has increased somewhat.

In 1991, all categories of mixed-aid finance rose substantially after three years of decline. Particularly strong increases were registered in aid with a concessionality level of 80 percent or more, although aid with a concessionality level of less than 50 percent still predominated (with a majority of aid finance containing a concessionality level of less than 80 percent).

V

Recent Developments in Financing from Multilateral Institutions

Multilateral institutions, including the IMF, have made substantial contributions to the financing of developing countries over the past decade. Their continued assistance has been a critical element in supporting the efforts of debtor countries implementing programs of adjustment and structural reform. Three trends stand out, which parallel those for official bilateral creditors. In the face of sharp reductions in financing from nonofficial sources, multilateral institutions have been providing an increasing share of new disbursements, especially to the low- and lower middle-income countries with debt-servicing difficulties. As a result, multilateral debt has increased rapidly over the past decade both in absolute terms and as a share of total debt. Second, the increase in multilateral lending—particularly policy-based lending in support of adjustment programs—has been most pronounced for countries that established a strong record of sustained policy performance. Third, multilateral institutions have increasingly adapted the terms of their lending to country circumstances with a marked shift toward concessional lending to low-income countries. The aggregate debt-service obligations of these countries to multilaterals have therefore increased only modestly despite the rapid rise in the share of their debt owed to multilaterals.

Coverage

In addition to the IMF, which is a monetary rather than a development institution, the most important multilateral lenders are the World Bank, comprising both the International Bank for Reconstruction and Development (IBRD) and the International Development Association (IDA); the three main regional development banks: the African Development Bank (AfDB), the Asian Development Bank (AsDB), and the Inter-American Development Bank (IDB); and a number of European multilateral financial institutions primarily associated with the European Community, such as the European Investment Bank and the Council of Europe.[31] Other multilateral lenders include institutions based in Arab countries (e.g., the Arab Fund for Economic and Social Develop-

ment and the OPEC Fund), and a large number of smaller regional organizations. Financing from multilateral institutions has been provided primarily in the form of loans, both nonconcessional and concessional (see Table A15).[32]

Lending by multilateral institutions is concentrated among the largest ten borrowers who together account for almost 50 percent of total multilateral exposure.[33] The three largest borrowers at the end of 1991 were India ($27.4 billion), Mexico ($22.2 billion), and Indonesia ($16.1 billion).[34]

Developments in Multilateral Debt

The total multilateral debt of all developing countries increased from $62 billion in 1980 to an estimated $270 billion by the end of 1992, (Chart 9 and Table A15). The World Bank is the most important multilateral creditor, and its loans constitute more than half of total multilateral debt. The total stock of developing country liabilities to the World Bank reached $150 billion at the end of 1992. Within this total, the share of concessional (IDA) loans has increased to about 35 percent in 1992, with the share being much higher for the low-income countries.

The share of the regional development banks in the stock of multilateral debt has risen from around 14 percent in 1987 to 21 percent in 1992. With a loan portfolio of $24 billion in 1992, the IDB remains the largest of the regional development banks in terms of debt outstanding and accounted for around 9 percent of total multilateral debt.[35]

---

[31]Over the next several years, the EBRD can also be expected to become a significant lender.

[32]Grants account for a relatively small share of total financing from these institutions. Grants, including those for humanitarian and technical assistance, have been provided mostly by the United Nations Development Program (UNDP) and various other agencies of the United Nations.

[33]The statistical information used in this section is derived mostly from the World Bank's Debtor Reporting System, supplemented with data from the OECD report *Geographical Distribution of Financial Flows to Developing Countries*, and Fund staff estimates.

[34]The next seven largest borrowers were Brazil ($12.3 billion), Turkey ($10.1 billion), Pakistan ($9.1 billion), Argentina ($7.9 billion), the Philippines ($7.8 billion), Bangladesh ($7.7 billion), and China ($7.6 billion).

[35]See Inter-American Development Bank, *Annual Report 1992* (Washington, 1993).

Table 15. Gross and Net Disbursements from Multilateral Institutions by Group of Countries, 1980–92[1]

(In millions of U.S. dollars)

		Annual Average 1980–86	1987	1988	1989	1990	1991	1992[2]
All countries	Gross	22,523	27,240	28,167	29,276	36,189	38,412	36,502
	Net	15,510	6,721	6,057	9,717	15,209	17,108	14,716
By region								
Sub-Saharan Africa	Gross	3,457	4,702	4,698	4,826	5,262	4,975	6,718
	Net	2,533	2,658	2,414	2,469	3,025	2,883	4,371
North Africa and the Middle East	Gross	1,444	2,422	2,209	3,050	2,463	3,329	3,230
	Net	896	1,046	759	1,668	705	1,367	1,089
Asia	Gross	7,137	8,790	9,448	9,794	11,038	12,500	12,506
	Net	5,139	2,198	2,831	4,563	4,982	7,046	7,643
Western Hemisphere	Gross	7,104	8,463	8,643	9,064	13,804	9,880	8,459
	Net	5,055	1,927	1,901	2,157	5,385	595	(999)
Other	Gross	3,120	2,793	3,116	2,527	3,598	7,733	4,549
	Net	1,887	(1,108)	(1,847)	(1,141)	1,101	5,217	2,611
By debt-servicing record								
Nonrescheduling countries	Gross	9,180	12,131	13,793	15,233	17,813	20,999	18,934
	Net	6,617	3,432	4,482	7,830	9,404	12,854	11,061
Rescheduling countries	Gross	13,056	15,108	14,374	14,043	18,376	17,412	17,569
	Net	8,894	3,288	1,576	1,886	5,805	4,254	3,554
Middle-income	Gross	10,876	12,476	11,753	11,490	15,352	14,403	13,742
	Net	7,366	1,724	51	531	4,164	2,505	944
Low-income	Gross	2,181	2,633	2,621	2,553	3,025	3,009	3,826
	Net	1,527	1,564	1,524	1,354	1,641	1,749	2,710
Memorandum item								
Selected ESAF countries[3]	Gross	1,343	2,251	2,374	2,151	2,548	2,600	2,563
	Net	1,031	1,383	1,464	1,352	1,551	1,832	1,852

Sources: World Bank Debtor Reporting System; and IMF staff estimates.

[1]Figures in parentheses are net repayments.

[2]Preliminary estimates.

[3]ESAF denotes enhanced structural adjustment facility. Countries include Bangladesh, Bolivia, the Gambia, Ghana, Guyana, Lesotho, Malawi, Mozambique, Senegal, Sri Lanka, and Togo.

However, the expansion of lending has been more rapid in the other two major regional development banks. Both the AsDB and the AfDB have doubled their share in total multilateral debt since 1987. At the end of 1992, the outstanding loan portfolio of the AsDB reached $21 billion,[36] while that of the AfDB amounted to $12 billion.[37] There has also been a significant increase in disbursements from multilateral institutions associated with the European Community over the past few years, in part reflecting larger assistance to Central and Eastern Europe.

A rapid increase in overall multilateral lending occurred during the first half of the 1980s when the

[36]See Asian Development Bank, *Annual Report 1992* (Manila, 1993).

[37]These data also include the African Development Fund. See African Development Bank, *Annual Report 1991* (Dakar, 1992).

developing countries were facing a particularly difficult situation (Table 15). Net lending averaged nearly $16 billion from 1990–92 compared with an average of $7.5 billion from 1987–89. Rising gross disbursements (which averaged $37 billion from 1990–92 compared with $28 billion in the previous three years) offset rising amortization payments. The continued increase in net financial support from multilateral institutions over this more recent period reflects largely the rapid expansion in lending to countries that have maintained their adjustment efforts. By contrast, countries that failed to implement consistently appropriate policies generally experienced a decline in multilateral lending. The link between policy performance and multilateral lending has been particularly marked in the case of policy-based adjustment lending, which has become a major component of multilateral assistance over the past decade. The IMF has always assisted countries in the design of comprehensive

Chart 9. Structure of Multilateral Debt of All Developing Countries by Institution, 1980–92[1]
(In billions of U.S. dollars)

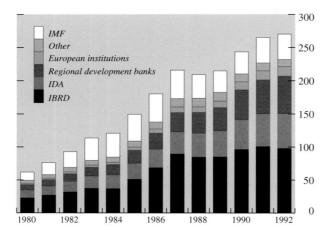

Sources: World Bank Debtor Reporting System; and IMF staff estimates.

Note: IBRD denotes International Bank for Reconstruction and Development; IDA denotes International Development Association.

[1]Data for 1992 are preliminary.

adjustment programs and made financial support contingent on the adoption and implementation of such programs. While project financing remains the main form of World Bank lending, the Bank has also provided substantial amounts through structural and sector adjustment loans in support of policy reforms; such loans accounted for over 25 percent of the World Bank's new commitments from 1986–92 (Table A18). The regional development banks have also provided policy-based financial assistance, though on a smaller scale, and have tended to follow the IMF and World Bank's lead.

The continued large-scale assistance over recent years in support of structural adjustment policies has helped to sustain the process of reform in a wide range of countries, and contributed to bringing a number of middle-income rescheduling countries to the point where they regained access to international capital markets. The IMF, the World Bank, and the IDB have also provided substantial support for commercial bank debt restructurings. Moreover, the World Bank's IDA debt-reduction facility has assisted low-income countries reduce debts to commercial banks and suppliers at steep discounts.[38]

Support from multilateral institutions has also played an important role in countries that have avoided debt-servicing difficulties (e.g., Bangladesh, India, Indonesia, Pakistan, and Tunisia). Financing packages supported by the multilateral institutions were decisive in assisting some countries that experienced a marked reduction in private lending avoid debt renegotiations (for example, Colombia in the mid-1980s, and Hungary in the late 1980s).[39] Similarly, multilateral financial assistance, including that through quick-disbursing adjustment loans, enabled a number of low-income countries that have generally implemented appropriate policies on a sustained basis to avoid debt reschedulings (notably, Burundi, and Ghana).

As a result of the rapid expansion of lending, the share of multilateral debt in total debt for all developing countries has been rising (Charts 9 and 10). This is particularly the case for rescheduling low- and lower middle-income countries, and in comparison to private creditors. In part, this reflects, in the case of middle-income countries, debt-reduction operations by commercial banks.

Lending to Low-Income Countries

During the recent past, multilateral lending to low-income countries (both rescheduling and non-rescheduling) has grown particularly rapidly as lending has expanded to countries implementing adjustment programs. In recognition of the deep-rooted balance of payments difficulties of many of these countries, and especially the low-income rescheduling countries, more lending was on concessional terms. This has been particularly marked in the case of the IMF, as financial support for the low-income countries has been provided since 1987 nearly exclusively in the form of disbursements under SAF and ESAF arrangements.

The World Bank converted many of the low-income countries to IDA-only status in the early 1980s; this prevented a buildup of debt on nonconcessional terms to the World Bank. The increase in the overall concessionality of World Bank lending during the 1980s is reflected in a changing composition of developing country debt to the World Bank (Chart 11). For example, within the group of low-income rescheduling countries, the share of IDA in the stock of debt owed to the World Bank increased significantly from 74 percent in 1987 to 90 percent in 1992 (Table A18). For selected countries that had ESAF arrangements with the IMF, and where sus-

---

[38]For details on commercial bank debt-reduction packages and the IDA debt-reduction facility see *Private Market Financing for Developing Countries*, World Economic and Financial Surveys (Washington: International Monetary Fund, December 1993).

[39]It is noteworthy that some countries have recently reduced reliance on multilateral lending (e.g., Colombia, Korea, Swaziland, Thailand), either because of expanding access to private financing on appropriate terms, or a declining overall reliance on external saving.

Chart 10. External Public Debt by Creditor, 1980–91

(In billions of U.S. dollars)

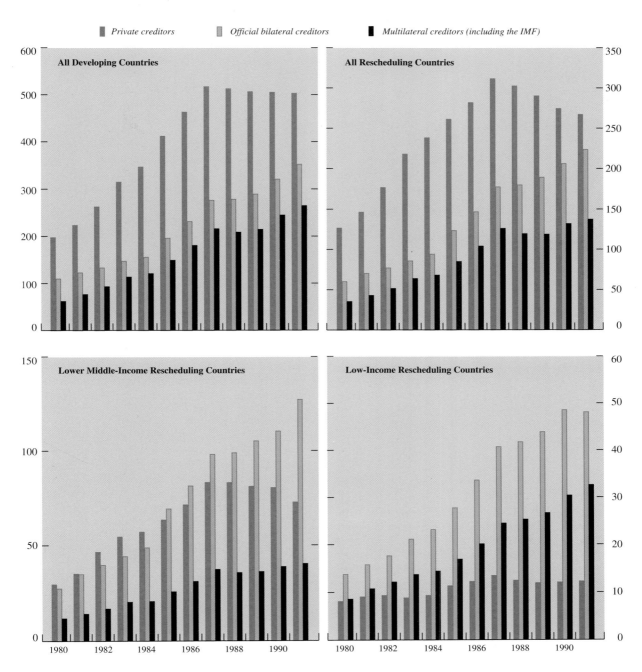

Sources: World Bank Debtor Reporting System; and IMF staff estimates.

Chart 11. Structure of Multilateral Debt by Lending Institution, 1980–92

(In billions of U.S. dollars)

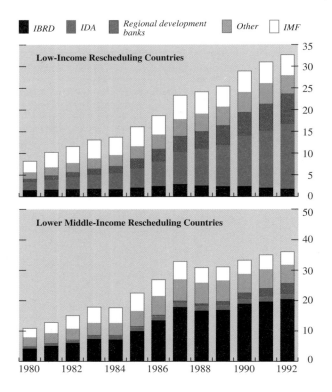

Sources: World Bank Debtor Reporting System; and IMF staff estimates.
Note: IBRD denotes International Bank for Reconstruction and Development; IDA denotes International Development Association.

Chart 12. Low-Income Rescheduling Countries: Concessionality of Multilateral Debt, 1980–92

(In billions of U.S. dollars)

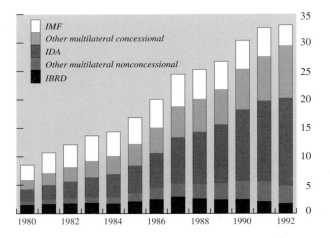

Sources: World Bank Debtor Reporting System; and IMF staff estimates.
Note: IBRD denotes International Bank for Reconstruction and Development; and IDA denotes International Development Association.

tained implementation of policy reforms was supported with increased lending on concessional terms, the share of IDA in total World Bank debt increased from 87 percent in 1987 to 95 percent in 1992.[40] The World Bank has also provided relief on the outstanding IBRD debt service for IDA-only countries through its Fifth Dimension facility. This facility has in recent years covered nearly 100 percent of IBRD interest payments due by IDA-only countries that have an adjustment program in

place.[41] There has also been more concessional lending from other multilaterals, in particular from the African Development Fund and the European institutions. Some multilateral institutions, however, have continued to provide resources in the form of nonconcessional lending. Chart 12 illustrates the rapid growth of highly concessional lending to the low-income rescheduling countries. It also shows the differences among multilateral institutions in the degree of concessionality.

Despite the rapid increase in the multilateral debt of the low-income countries, debt-service obligations have increased only modestly in recent years mostly as the result of the marked shift toward concessional assistance, especially on the part of the IMF and the World Bank. For low-income rescheduling countries as a group, the debt-service ratio on multilateral debt, including the IMF, has remained at around 10 percent of exports of goods

---

[40]These countries, which include Bangladesh, Bolivia, The Gambia, Ghana, Guyana, Lesotho, Malawi, Mozambique, Senegal, Sri Lanka, and Togo, were identified in a recent review by IMF staff as having made visible progress toward external viability. See, Susan Schadler, and others, *Economic Adjustment in Low-Income Countries: Experience Under Enhanced Structural Adjustment Facility*, Occasional Paper, No. 106 (Washington: International Monetary Fund, September 1993).

[41]Supplementary fast-disbursing IDA credits are made available under the Fifth Dimension facility to IDA-only countries with outstanding IBRD obligations (i.e., "reverse graduates"), in order to ease their debt-service burdens. To be eligible, countries must be implementing an IDA-supported program of structural adjustment. The total amount of such financing available each year is decided by IDA's Executive Board in the context of allocating IDA reflow resources. Fifth Dimension resources are prorated among eligible countries; disbursements are made once a year alongside the release of a tranche under an adjustment credit. (If the tranche release is delayed, the supplementary credit may be carried forward for up to 12 months.)

Chart 13. Low-Income Countries: Debt-Service Payments on Multilateral Debt, 1984–92[1]

(In percent of exports of goods and services)

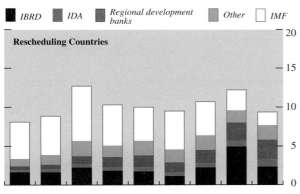

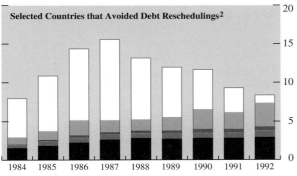

Sources: World Bank Debtor Reporting System; and IMF staff estimates.

Note: IBRD denotes International Bank for Reconstruction and Development; IDA denotes International Development Association.

[1]Payments actually made.

[2]See Table A22 for listing of countries.

Table 16. Structure of Multilateral Debt for Selected Developing Countries, 1984 and 1992

| | Percentage of Total Multilateral Debt on Concessional Terms | |
	1984	1992
Low-income rescheduling countries	52.4	76.0
Selected low-income countries that avoided reschedulings	57.1	76.4
Lower middle-income rescheduling countries	29.3	18.2

Sources: World Bank Debtor Reporting System; and IMF staff estimates.

and services (upper panel of Chart 13). However, these aggregate figures mask a wide range of country circumstances (Table A20).[42] For low-income countries that avoided debt reschedulings as a group, debt-service ratios have been higher over most of the period with a peak of over 15 percent in 1987, followed by a steady decline to some 9 percent in 1992 (lower panel of Chart 13).

New disbursements from multilateral institutions exceeded by a wide margin debt-service payments on multilateral debt for both rescheduling and non-

rescheduling low-income countries. For the low-income rescheduling countries as a group, total multilateral disbursements (excluding the IMF) over the period 1989–91 were equivalent to some 23 percent of exports of goods and services compared with debt-service payments (including the IMF) of around 10 percent (see Table 14). Disbursements, including those from the IMF, averaged $3 billion a year from 1989–91 (Table A20). Thus, the proportion of multilateral debt on concessional terms rose from around one half in 1984 to three fourths in 1992 (Chart 12, Table 16, and Table A22). The nonrescheduling low-income countries witnessed a similar pattern of disbursements (Table A22); the percentage of concessional debt also rose from 57 percent in 1984 to 76 percent in 1992 (Tables 17 and A23).[43]

The recent experience of low-income countries reveals the strong link between policy performance and external financial support. Countries that achieved improvements in their macroeconomic and structural policies continued to receive significant net disbursements from the multilateral institutions on increasingly concessional terms. In contrast, countries with an uneven record of policy implementation (some of which faced very difficult economic and political situations) experienced difficulties in obtaining financial support. More generally, both official multilateral and bilateral creditors and donors have provided increased levels of financial assistance where sustained adjustment and reform efforts by the debtor countries have provided assurances that resources would be efficiently used.

---

[42]It should also be noted that these figures are based on payments actually made and thus do not take into account arrears accumulation.

[43]By contrast, the percentage share of concessional debt for lower middle-income rescheduling countries declined from 29 percent in 1984 to 18 percent in 1992 (Tables 17 and A24).

Appendix I

Framework of Multilateral Official Debt Renegotiations

Multilateral official debt renegotiations deal with the rescheduling of debt-service payments on loans extended by, or guaranteed by, the governments or the official agencies of the participating creditor countries. They are normally, though not exclusively, undertaken under the aegis of the Paris Club. The Club has neither a fixed membership nor an institutional structure; rather it represents a set of practices and procedures that has evolved since the first ad hoc meeting for Argentina in 1956. Meetings are open to all official creditors that accept those practices and procedures.

The rescheduling exercise is initiated by the debtor country sending a formal request for a meeting to the Chairman of the Paris Club (who, by tradition, is an official of the French Treasury). The debtor supplies a breakdown of external debt-service payments, by creditor; on this basis the Chairman, in consultation with the debtor, sends invitations for a meeting to individual creditor countries. The Fund, the World Bank, the United Nations Conference on Trade and Development, and, where relevant, the regional development bank concerned are invited to make presentations at the meeting. Official creditors meet with the debtor to negotiate an agreement (the Agreed Minute) that is then signed ad referendum by all creditor countries attending the meeting unless the amounts to be covered by the rescheduling agreement are less than the de minimis level, in which case creditor countries do not reschedule but may attend as observers.

The Agreed Minute sets out the broad terms of rescheduling that the participants recommend for the subsequent bilateral agreements between the debtor and each creditor country. These bilateral agreements form the legal basis for the debt rescheduling and establish the interest rates on the debt rescheduled. The date by which such agreements are to be signed is specified in the Minute.

Official creditors require two preconditions for the initiation of a debt renegotiation. They must be convinced, first, that the debtor country will be unable to meet its external payments obligations unless it receives debt relief and, second, that the debtor country will take the steps necessary to eliminate the causes of its payments difficulties and to achieve a durable improvement in its external payments position. Creditors rely on the Fund to help member countries design appropriate adjustment measures and generally require that an upper credit tranche arrangement with the Fund be in place before debt renegotiations are initiated. Since early 1987, Paris Club creditors have also accepted arrangements under the structural adjustment facility (SAF), the enhanced structural adjustment facility (ESAF), and rights accumulation program (RAP) as evidence of appropriate adjustment policies being undertaken.

Official debt reschedulings typically cover both principal and interest payments on medium- and long-term debt falling due during a given period (the consolidation period); where necessary, creditors also covered payments already in arrears at the beginning of the consolidation period, especially with countries undertaking reschedulings with official creditors for the first time. During the past decade an important factor determining Paris Club practices on coverage has been the increasing recognition by both debtors and creditors of the link between Paris Club reschedulings and the stance of cover policies of export credit agencies. Creditors have implemented a strategy of subordination aimed at minimizing the effects of reschedulings on new financial assistance from official creditors. The most important element in this strategy has been the firm maintenance since May 1984 of established cutoff dates in the rescheduling agreements with Fund member countries seeking successive reschedulings. Creditors also have a long-standing policy to exclude debt service on short-term debt from reschedulings, and debtor countries have increasingly requested the exclusion of debts contracted by the private sector of the rescheduling countries.

Paris Club agreements have also excluded all debts contracted by binational or multinational entities or guaranteed by a third party, for example, a nonresident corporation or a government other than that of the debtor or creditor. Rental and lease payments are excluded as well. Apart from these, Paris Club principles do not permit the exclusion of any other types of bilateral debt from the rescheduling agreement. In the past, some debtor countries have requested other exclusions but, primarily for reasons of precedent and intercreditor equity, official creditors have refused to accede to such requests. In particular, creditors have reaffirmed that secured debts, debts repayable in commodities, and debts covered by special payment mechanisms (such as escrow accounts) are subject to the provisions of the Agreed Minute and that no distinction is to be made between buyers' and suppliers' credit.

Implementation of Agreed Minute

While the Agreed Minute sets out the general terms of the debt restructuring, except with regard to interest rates, the bilateral agreements concluded between the debtor country and each creditor country are the legal basis implementing the restructuring. Some creditor countries require, in addition to a framework bilateral agreement, that the debtor country conclude individual agreements implementing that bilateral with various national lending agencies involved in the rescheduling.

Under the provisions contained in the Agreed Minute, the debtor country is expected to conclude the bilateral agreements with each creditor country without undue delay and, in any case, by the bilateral deadline. The period between the date of the Agreed Minute and the bilateral deadline has averaged close to seven months in recent years. Official creditors will normally not agree to a meeting on a new rescheduling until the bilateral agreements implementing the previous Agreed Minute have been signed. For a variety of reasons, debtor countries have often failed to conclude bilateral agreements by the deadline specified in the Agreed Minute. Sometimes administrative problems have arisen in setting a mutually convenient schedule for bilateral negotiations, particularly when a relatively large number of creditors is involved. In other instances, some major creditor countries have participated in a large number of Paris Club reschedulings in the past several years and have had to negotiate a correspondingly large number of bilateral agreements. In addition, difficult technical and legal issues have sometimes arisen in the compilation and verification of the relevant data and claims. This has been a problem for first reschedulings, in particular, in cases with long-standing arrears. The reconciliation of data on short-term trade arrears has been particularly difficult. Also, in some cases, there have been protracted negotiations on the interest rates to be applied to rescheduled amounts.

On occasion, despite the best efforts by the debtor country in negotiating with creditors, delays in the completion of a few of the bilateral agreements have occurred; in these instances, the official creditors concerned have generally been willing to proceed with a new consolidation. In such instances, the effectiveness of the new Agreed Minute may be conditional upon the conclusion of outstanding bilateral agreements under the previous Agreed Minute.

Since interest rates are not determined until bilateral agreements are negotiated, the debtor typically does not begin to make moratorium interest payments until then. This results in a bunching of interest payments that otherwise would have been spread over the consolidation period. When obligations on the rescheduled debt accumulated to a point where the debtor was unable to make the required payments following the signature of the bilateral agreements, this bunching has created problems. In some instances this may have reflected unforeseen external factors, but in other cases it was due to policy slippages in the implementation of the adjustment programs. Moreover, the emergence of new external payments arrears had serious implications under the Fund arrangement. To facilitate the implementation of the Agreed Minute, certain debtor countries have, therefore, agreed to establish a special account with a central bank of one of the participating creditor countries into which monthly deposits would be placed. The overall amount is calculated to approximate the amounts payable to all participating creditors during the consolidation period. While regular servicing of a special account can send a positive signal to official creditors, the establishment of a special account alone has not ensured the full implementation of the Agreed Minute, as some debtor countries have failed to make the required monthly deposits.

All Paris Club Agreed Minutes include provisions that govern the payment of nonrescheduled debts to Paris Club creditors. The provisions stipulate that nonrescheduled amounts should be paid as scheduled but no later than by a specified date. This date has generally been set about three months after the date of the Agreed Minute, but has been extended significantly in some cases. Nonrescheduled amounts include, notably, post-cutoff date debt and debt to creditors that are de minimis as well as debts not covered by the Agreed Minute.

Appendix II

Glossary of Selected Terms in Multilateral Official Debt Reschedulings

Agreed Minute—The terms agreed upon in the multilateral rescheduling meeting are embodied in an Agreed Minute. The Minute normally specifies the coverage of debt-service payments to be consolidated, the cutoff date, the consolidation period, the proportion of payments to be rescheduled, the provisions regarding the down payment, and the repayment scheduled for both the rescheduled and deferred debt. Delegates to the meeting undertake to recommend to their governments the incorporation of these terms in the bilateral agreements that implement the rescheduling.

Arrears—unpaid amounts that fell due before the beginning of the consolidation period.

Bilateral agreements—Agreements reached bilaterally between the debtor country and agencies in each of the participating creditor countries; these establish the legal basis of the debt restructuring set forth in the Agreed Minute. Bilateral agreements specify the interest rate on amounts deferred or rescheduled (moratorium interest), which is agreed bilaterally between the debtor and each creditor.

Bilateral deadline—the date by which all bilateral agreements must be concluded. The period for concluding bilateral agreements is now generally six to seven months from the date of the Agreed Minute.

"Blended payments"—refers to the graduated repayment schedule for principal payments with extended overall maturities (up to 14 years from the previous 10 years), but a shorter grace period, granted to upper-middle-income countries since February 1992.

Concessional rescheduling—See below, enhanced concessions and Toronto terms.

Conditional further rescheduling—See below, "multiyear rescheduling agreement."

Consolidated amounts—the debt service payments and arrears rescheduled under a rescheduling agreement.

Consolidation period—the period in which debt-service payments to be consolidated or rescheduled under the terms applicable to current maturities have fallen or will fall due. The beginning of the consolidation period may precede, coincide with, or come after the date of the Agreed Minute.

Coverage—the amount of eligible debt service or arrears covered by the rescheduling agreement. Comprehensive coverage implies the inclusion of most or all eligible debt service and arrears.

Current maturities—principal and interest payments falling due within the consolidation period.

Cutoff date—the date before which loans must have been contracted in order for their debt service to be covered by the rescheduling. Decisions about whether to include in an agreement debt service due under previous multilateral official reschedulings are made independently of whether those previous agreements were before or after the cutoff date.

Cutoff interval—the number of months between the cutoff date and the beginning of the consolidation period.

"De minimis" clause—the provision whereby creditor countries whose claims are less than a specified minimum amount are excluded from the rescheduling agreement. Since 1983, about one half of the agreements have provided limits of SDR 500,000 or SDR 250,000. The debtor is expected to pay all claims excluded by this clause. Overdue claims are to be paid as soon as possible, and in any case by a date specified in the Agreed Minute.

Debt-reduction option—see enhanced concessions.

Debt-service-reduction option—see enhanced concessions.

Debt-subordination strategy—the policy of the Paris Club under which new loans (contracted after the cutoff date) are excluded from rescheduling agreements. (Pre-cutoff date loans are subordinate to post-cutoff loans).

Debt-swap operations—voluntary operations under which a creditor agrees that a certain debt is serviced by the debtor in domestic currency which can be used for equity purchase or environmental projects. No limits on swaps apply for ODA or direct government loans; but for other loans they are limited (under Paris Club agreements) to the higher of $10 million or 10 percent of consolidated commercial credits.

Deferred payments—arrears or debt-service obligations that are not rescheduled under the terms of the Agreed Minute but are postponed. The Agreed Minute specifies a repayment schedule for these obligations; for arrears on post-cutoff date debt, full repayment is generally required during the consolidation period.

Down payment—In this paper, down payment refers to payments falling due within the consolidation period on debts covered by the agreement.

Enhanced concessions—refers to the exceptional rescheduling terms granted, since December 1991, to the poorest and most heavily indebted countries. The new menu incorporating enhanced concessions provides for a 50 percent reduction (in net present value terms) of debt-service payments consolidated on non-ODA debts through two main options. Under the first option, debt reduction, 50 percent of the debt service consolidated is canceled; the remainder is rescheduled at market interest rates over 23 years with a graduated repayment schedule including a grace period of 6 years. Under the second option, debt-service reduction, the amount of debt service consolidated is rescheduled at reduced interest rates so as to reduce the net present value by 50 percent; principal payments are graduated over 23 years with no grace period. The menu includes a variant of the latter option that combines a lesser reduction of interest rates with a partial capitalization of moratorium interest, also providing a 50 percent present value reduction. The menu also includes the nonconcessional option B under "Toronto terms" (the long-maturities option) under which the debt service consolidated is rescheduled on the basis of the appropriate market rate over 25 years, including a grace period of 16 years (14 years prior to June 1992). As regards concessional ODA loans, creditors provide for graduated payments over 30 years (including a grace period of 12 years) at concessional interest rates. The rescheduling agreements based on the new menu contain the provision that Paris Club creditors would be willing to consider the matter of the stock of debt after a period of 3–4 years. For such consideration, the debtor country must have fully implemented the earlier rescheduling agreement, made comparable debt-relief arrangements with other creditors, and continued an appropriate arrangement with the IMF.

Effectively rescheduled portion—the proportion of total payments covered by the rescheduling agreement that is rescheduled or otherwise deferred until after the end of the consolidation period.

Flow rescheduling—the rescheduling of specified debt service falling due during the consolidation period. This, together with the rescheduling in some cases of the stock of specified arrears outstanding at the beginning of the consolidation period, has been the approach used in all Paris Club reschedulings so far, except in the cases of Egypt and Poland in 1991.

Goodwill clause—refers to creditors' willingness as expressed in the Agreed Minute to meet to consider a further debt rescheduling in the future, subject to fulfillment by the debtor country of certain specified conditions.

Grace period and maturity—Paris Club Agreed Minutes specify the first and last payment dates, but do not refer to the length of the grace period or to the maturity. In this paper, grace periods and maturity on rescheduled current maturities are counted from the end of the consolidation period. In the case of the rescheduling of arrears and late interest on arrears, they are measured from the beginning of the consolidation period.

Graduated payments—see blended payments.

Graduation—debtor countries graduate from the Paris Club when they cease relying on reschedulings from Paris Club creditors.

Initiative clause—the standard undertaking in the Agreed Minute that the debtor country will seek to restructure debts owed to other creditors on terms comparable to those outlined in the Agreed Minute. This clause appears as one of the general recommendations and reads:

In order to secure comparable treatment of public and private external creditors on their debts, the Delegation of [debtor country] stated that their Government will seek to secure from external creditors, including banks and suppliers, rescheduling or refinancing arrangements on terms comparable to those set forth in this Agreed Minute for credits of comparable maturity, making sure to avoid inequity between different categories of creditors.

Late interest—interest accrued on principal and interest in arrears.

Local currency clause—refers to a provision in the Agreed Minute (normally in cases where private debt is rescheduled) whereby the debtor country undertakes to establish or extend the necessary mechanisms to ensure that debtors other than the Government can make into the central bank or other appropriate institutions the local currency counterpart payments corresponding on the due dates.

Long-maturities option—nonconcessional option under enhanced concessions under which the consolidated amount is rescheduled over 25 years with 16 years grace (14 years prior to June 1992).

Low-income countries—poorest, most heavily indebted countries eligible to receive "enhanced concessions" terms. The Paris Club has decided eligibility on a case-by-case basis. Only countries eligible to receive highly concessional IDA credits from the World Bank ("IDA only") have been deemed low-income.

"Lower middle-income country terms" (LMIC)—refers to the rescheduling terms granted, since September 1990, to the most heavily indebted lower middle-income countries. These terms provide for 15-year maturities with a grace period of up to 8 years for commercial credits, compared with the standard rescheduling terms of 10 years with 5–6 years grace. ODA credits are rescheduled over 20 years including a grace period of up to 10 years. This set of rescheduling terms also includes the introduction—on a voluntary basis—of the limited use of debt swaps.

Maturity—grace period plus repayment period.

Middle-income countries—countries not considered lower middle-income or low-income by the Paris Club. They receive standard terms (rescheduling over 10 years, with 5–6 years' grace) from the Paris Club.

Moratorium interest—the interest payments on the amounts rescheduled (the consolidated amounts) or deferred under the agreement. These are specified in the bilateral agreements.

Most-favored-nation clause—the standard undertaking in the Agreed Minute whereby the debtor country agrees not to accord to creditor countries that did not participate in the multilateral agreement repayment terms more favorable than those accorded to the participating creditor countries for the consolidation of debts of comparable term.

Multiyear rescheduling agreement (MYRA)—agreements, granted by official creditors, that cover consolidation periods of two or more years. They are implemented through a succession of shorter consolidations (serial reschedulings) that automatically come into effect after certain conditions are satisfied or tranched consolidations. To this effect, the Agreed Minute includes provisions that set forth the payments due in specified future periods, and the conditions for such a rescheduling to become effective without a further Paris Club meeting. The implementation of each stage requires only a decision by creditors that the relevant conditions have been met. The conditions generally include full implementation to date of the rescheduling agreement and implementation of IMF-supported programs.

Serial rescheduling—see "multiyear rescheduling agreement."

Special account—an account established under some Agreed Minutes by the debtor country with the central bank of a participating creditor country into which monthly deposits of an agreed amount are made. The total amount deposited usually approximates the amounts estimated to be payable to all participating creditors during the year; the debtor country draws on the account as bilateral implementing agreements are signed and specific payments under these agreements become due.

Standard terms—the standard rescheduling terms offered by the Paris Club to middle-income countries, under which the consolidated amounts are rescheduled (at market rates) over 10 years with a grace period of 5–6 years. ODA credits receive the same terms.

Stock-of-debt operation—rescheduling of the eligible stock of debt outstanding as opposed to flow reschedulings. Stock-of-debt operations by the Paris Club have occurred, only on an exceptional basis, in the cases of Egypt and Poland in 1991. Under enhanced concessions, the Paris Club has agreed to consider stock-of-debt operations for low-income countries provided certain conditions are met.

"Toronto terms"—(the options approach) the rescheduling granted, between October 1988 and June 1991, to the poorest and most heavily indebted countries. Under this approach, creditors chose one of three options (or a combination of options). Under Option A (partial cancellation), one third of debt-service obligations consolidated was canceled and the remaining two thirds rescheduled on the basis of the appropriate market rate over 14 years, including a grace period of 8 years. Under Option B (extended maturities), debt-service obligations consolidated were rescheduled on the basis of the appropriate market rate over 25 years, including a grace period of 14 years. Under Option C (concessional interest rates), debt-service obligations consolidated were rescheduled over 14 years, including a grace period of 8 years on the basis of the appropriate market rate reduced by 3.5 percent.

Transfer clause—a provision in the Agreed Minute that commits the debtor government to guarantee the immediate and unrestricted transfer of foreign exchange in all cases where the private sector pays the local currency counterpart for servicing its debt to Paris Club creditors.

Appendix III
Statistical Tables

Table A1. Selected Lower Middle-Income Rescheduling Countries: Balance of Payments and Debt Indicators, 1986–92[1]

	1986	1987	1988	1989	1990	1991	1992
	(In billions of U.S. dollars)						
Exports	52.2	56.2	60.8	63.8	70.6	63.3	64.8
Imports	60.2	64.6	69.1	69.8	74.3	71.3	78.9
Trade balance	−8.0	−8.4	−8.3	−6.0	−3.7	−8.0	−14.1
Net services (excluding scheduled interest)	2.4	4.3	4.3	2.8	4.9	6.5	7.2
Scheduled interest payments	12.8	15.1	16.7	18.0	19.4	19.6	15.5
Private transfers	6.1	6.9	7.5	7.4	9.0	8.2	9.2
Official transfers	2.3	1.4	2.5	3.0	5.6	4.3	3.5
Current account balance	−10.0	−10.9	−10.7	−10.8	−3.6	−8.6	−9.7
Medium- and long-term borrowing	−8.2	−11.0	−10.8	−8.9	−12.7	−11.8	−9.1
Disbursements	9.3	10.1	9.7	9.9	10.1	9.6	8.8
Amortization	−17.5	−21.1	−20.5	−18.8	−22.8	−21.4	−17.9
Other capital, net	5.1	1.2	2.1	2.7	2.7	4.9	5.7
Overall balance	−13.1	−20.7	−19.4	−17.0	−13.6	−15.5	−13.1
Reserve, net (− increase)	−1.2	1.0	−1.6	−2.8	−11.8	−7.4	−6.1
IMF, net	−0.6	−0.7	−0.6	−0.4	−0.3	0.6	—
Exceptional financing	14.3	19.7	21.0	19.8	25.4	22.9	19.2
Memorandum items							
Noninterest current surplus[2]	0.5	2.8	3.5	4.2	10.2	6.7	2.3
Scheduled debt service[3]	31.3	37.6	38.4	37.9	43.4	41.9	34.8
Actual debt service	17.0	17.9	17.4	18.1	18.0	19.0	15.6
Total external debt[3]	206.6	227.5	236.4	247.6	256.4	262.5	259.9
Share in gross financing							
Grants	8.9	4.5	7.5	9.2	13.6	11.7	11.1
Disbursements	35.9	32.4	29.2	30.3	24.6	26.1	27.9
Exceptional financing	55.2	63.1	63.2	60.6	61.8	62.2	61.0
Terms of trade (1980=100)	86.2	81.6	84.2	84.8	79.4	77.8	76.1
	(In percent of exports of goods and services)						
Total external debt[3]	329.0	334.9	326.1	326.4	287.7	324.1	304.0
Gross financing	41.2	45.9	45.8	43.1	46.1	45.4	36.8
Scheduled debt service[3]	49.8	55.4	53.0	49.9	48.7	51.7	40.0
Interest	20.4	22.2	23.0	23.7	21.8	24.2	18.1
Amortization	29.5	33.2	30.0	26.2	26.9	27.5	21.9
Actual debt service	27.1	26.4	24.0	23.8	20.2	23.4	17.5

Source: IMF staff estimates.
[1]Countries are listed in Table A2.
[2]Balance on goods and services and private transfers, excluding interest payments.
[3]Including the IMF.

Table A2. Selected Lower Middle-Income Rescheduling Countries: Structure of External Financing, 1986 and 1992

(In percent of exports of goods and services)

	Noninterest Current Account (surplus −)	Total Scheduled Debt Service[1]	Financing				
			Total	Grants	Disburse-ments	Exceptional	Other[2]
Group 1: Improving situation			**1986**				
Costa Rica	−13	63	50	8	21	29	−8
Dominican Republic	−3	48	45	2	11	19	13
Ecuador	−7	81	74	2	37	45	−10
Egypt	24	73	97	17	43	18	19
Jamaica	−21	77	56	2	18	21	15
Morocco	−19	114	95	—	38	55	2
Philippines	−33	51	18	2	16	19	−23
Poland	−15	54	39	—	9	33	−3
Average	−11	70	59	4	24	30	−1
Group 2: Deteriorating situation							
Bulgaria	14	15	29	—	—	—	29
Cameroon	14	16	30	3	10	—	17
Congo	56	66	122	8	25	41	48
Côte d'Ivoire	−5	39	34	2	10	11	11
Jordan	14	19	33	20	15	—	−2
Nigeria	32	71	103	−2	12	45	48
Peru	8	78	86	4	16	53	13
Average	19	43	62	5	13	21	23
Group 1: Improving situation			**1992**				
Costa Rica	9	19	28	2	14	—	12
Dominican Republic	−4	24	20	4	7	4	5
Ecuador	−11	65	54	3	14	30	7
Egypt	−22	24	2	13	14	—	−25
Jamaica	−9	33	24	3	11	4	6
Morocco	−11	45	34	—	24	9	1
Philippines	−2	26	24	5	15	9	−5
Poland	−10	19	9	2	3	9	−5
Average	−8	32	24	4	13	6	1
Group 2: Deteriorating situation							
Bulgaria	−3	51	48	—	3	44	1
Cameroon	18	43	61	—	6	35	20
Congo	20	57	77	2	13	35	27
Côte d'Ivoire	11	62	73	5	23	39	6
Jordan	14	42	56	10	6	16	24
Nigeria	−13	69	56	—	4	38	14
Peru	13	58	71	7	17	49	−2
Average	9	55	64	4	11	37	12

Source: IMF staff estimates.

[1]Including the IMF.

[2]Including other net capital flows and change in net reserves (increase −), including IMF purchases and disbursements.

Table A3. Low-Income Rescheduling Countries: Balance of Payments and Debt Indicators, 1986–92

	1986	1987	1988	1989	1990	1991	1992
	(In billions of U.S. dollars)						
Exports	11.9	13.0	14.1	15.2	15.5	15.2	15.2
Imports	15.1	16.5	17.9	17.9	18.7	18.5	19.9
Trade balance	−3.2	−3.5	−3.7	−2.7	−3.2	−3.3	−4.7
Net services (excluding scheduled interest)	−3.0	−2.8	−3.6	−3.9	−4.1	−4.8	−5.2
Scheduled interest payments	−3.3	−3.6	−4.0	−4.4	−4.6	−4.6	−4.5
Private transfers	1.0	1.3	1.4	1.2	0.9	1.0	1.2
Official transfers	4.2	4.1	4.5	5.0	5.2	5.5	6.4
Current account balance	−4.3	−4.4	−5.5	−4.8	−5.8	−6.3	−6.8
Medium-and long-term borrowing	0.5	0.5	0.4	−0.1	−0.5	−1.4	−2.1
Disbursements	5.4	5.4	5.6	5.6	5.4	5.4	5.1
Amortization	−4.9	−4.9	−5.2	−5.7	−5.9	−6.8	−7.2
Other capital, net	−0.7	−1.4	−0.7	−1.4	−0.2	0.6	1.6
Overall balance	−4.5	−5.3	−5.8	−6.3	−6.6	−7.1	−7.3
Reserves, net (− increase)	−0.5	−0.1	−0.3	−0.2	−0.1	−0.7	−1.0
IMF net	−0.2	−0.1	−0.2	−0.2	−0.2	—	0.2
Exceptional financing	5.1	5.4	6.0	6.5	6.7	7.7	8.3
Memorandum items							
Noninterest current account deficit[1]	5.2	5.0	6.0	5.4	6.4	7.2	8.7
Scheduled debt service[2]	9.1	9.0	9.7	10.8	11.2	11.7	12.0
Actual debt service[2]	4.0	3.7	3.7	4.3	4.5	4.0	3.6
Total external debt[2]	69.0	82.5	88.1	89.8	100.0	102.4	104.1
Share in gross financing							
Grants	28.6	27.5	28.1	29.3	30.1	29.5	32.2
Disbursements	36.7	36.2	34.6	32.7	31.0	29.1	25.8
Exceptional financing	34.7	36.3	37.3	38.0	38.8	41.4	42.0
Terms of trade (1980 = 100)	105.3	98.5	95.4	93.8	91.5	90.5	88.5
	(In percent of exports of goods and services)						
Total external debt[2]	479.4	538.2	533.9	511.0	536.0	556.5	555.1
Gross financing	102.1	97.2	97.4	97.3	92.5	101.1	105.5
Scheduled debt service[2]	62.9	59.6	59.1	61.5	60.1	63.8	63.8
Interest	22.9	23.3	24.1	25.0	24.7	25.0	24.0
Amortization	40.0	36.3	35.0	36.5	35.4	38.8	39.8
Actual debt service[2]	27.5	24.3	22.7	24.5	24.1	21.9	19.5

Source: IMF staff estimates.

[1]Balance on goods and services and private transfers, excluding scheduled interest payments.

[2]Including the IMF.

Table A4. Low-Income Rescheduling Countries: Structure of External Financing, 1986

(In percent of exports of goods and services)

	Noninterest Current Account Deficit (−: surplus)	Total Scheduled Debt Service[1]	Financing				
			Total	Grants	Disbursements	Exceptional	Other[2]
Angola	14	35	49	4	25	18	2
Benin	15	28	43	9	14	21	−1
Bolivia	17	83	100	11	32	48	9
Burkina Faso	102	35	137	103	42	14	−22
Central African Republic	79	22	101	52	51	5	−7
Chad	164	12	176	129	16	2	29
Equatorial Guinea	63	51	114	69	23	18	4
Ethiopia	43	31	74	43	68	—	−37
Gambia, The	25	49	74	39	8	25	2
Guinea	16	36	52	7	29	10	6
Guinea-Bissau	332	89	421	239	100	26	56
Guyana	26	81	107	2	26	61	18
Honduras	9	35	44	14	32	11	−13
Madagascar	11	81	92	27	48	40	−23
Malawi	6	63	69	—	59	20	−10
Mali	121	47	168	69	62	22	15
Mauritania	46	45	91	24	29	19	19
Mozambique	236	247	483	108	143	243	−11
Nicaragua	189	329	518	38	213	292	−25
Niger	33	49	82	41	31	15	−5
Senegal	29	37	66	17	38	11	—
Sierra Leone	6	89	95	20	13	58	4
Somalia	318	161	479	261	133	116	−31
Sudan	33	108	141	48	22	77	−6
Tanzania	76	70	146	65	37	48	−4
Togo	21	30	51	20	17	3	11
Uganda	−15	63	48	8	58	1	−19
Zaïre	6	51	57	9	19	20	9
Zambia	9	95	104	21	39	63	−19
Average	70	74	144	54	48	45	−2
Total	36	63	99	29	38	35	−3

Source: IMF staff estimates.

[1]Including the IMF.

[2]Including other net capital flows and change in net reserves (increase −), including IMF purchases and disbursements.

Table A5. Selected Low-Income Rescheduling Countries: Structure of Debt-Service Payments, 1992

(In percent of exports of goods and services)[1]

	Scheduled Debt Service								
	Nonrestructurable debt					Restructurable debt[2]			
		Of which					Of which		
Country	Total (1)	IMF (2)	Other multilateral (3)	Post-cutoff (4)	Other[3] (5)	Total (6)	Interest (7)	Principal (8)	Total (9)
Angola	6	—	—	3	3	39	11	28	45
Benin	6	—	5	—	1	31	10	21	37
Bolivia	30	6	22	1	2	29	9	19	58
Burkina Faso	11	—	9	—	2	5	2	3	16
Central African Republic	14	3	6	2	3	10	2	8	25
Ethiopia	22	—	8	—	14	44	8	36	66
Guinea	12	2	4	1	5	17	5	12	29
Guyana	19	1	13	3	2	41	15	26	60
Honduras	24	1	21	—	2	20	10	11	44
Madagascar	25	4	11	2	9	57	17	40	82
Mali	10	2	6	—	2	36	6	30	46
Mauritania	20	2	13	1	4	19	5	14	39
Mozambique	25	1	6	5	13	134	35	99	160
Nicaragua	38	1	27	1	10	326	70	256	364
Niger	13	3	7	3	—	16	6	11	30
Senegal	13	3	6	2	2	11	5	6	24
Sierra Leone	17	6	4	1	7	15	6	9	32
Tanzania	14	1	9	—	4	29	10	20	43
Togo	7	3	3	—	1	14	5	8	21
Uganda	71	14	27	5	25	39	27	12	110
Zaïre	16	5	7	2	2	80	33	47	96
Zambia	38	8	12	3	15	26	6	20	64

Source: IMF staff estimates.

Note: Totals may not add due to rounding.

[1]The debt-service structure for 1992 is broadly representative of the debt-service profile over the medium term. Liberia, Somalia, and Sudan are excluded because of data limitations.

[2]Includes pre-cutoff date debt to Paris Club, other official bilateral, and private creditors.

[3]Includes short-term debt and other debt that have been excluded explicitly or implicitly from rescheduling, such as private sector debts, as well as debt service from previous concessional rescheduling on Toronto terms and on enhanced concessions.

Table A6. Status of Paris Club Rescheduling Countries as of June 30, 1993
(Dates refer to end of current or last consolidation period)

Graduated Countries		Rescheduling Agreements in Effect		Rescheduling Agreements Not in Effect	
Low-income countries[1]					
Gambia, The	9/87	*Benin	12/95	Angola	9/90
Malawi	5/89	*Bolivia	6/93	Central African Republic	12/90
		*Burkina Faso	12/95	Chad	12/90
		*Ethiopia	10/95	*Equatorial Guinea	12/92
		*Guyana	12/94	*Guinea	12/92[2]
		*Honduras	7/95	Guinea-Bissau	12/90
		*Mali	8/95	Liberia	6/85
		*Mauritania	12/94	Madagascar	6/91
		*Mozambique	12/94	*Nicaragua	3/93
		*Sierra Leone	2/94	Niger	12/91
		*Tanzania	6/94	Senegal	6/92
		*Togo	6/94	Somalia	12/88
		*Uganda	11/93	Sudan	12/84
		*Zambia	3/95	Zaïre	6/90
Lower middle-income countries[3]					
Dominican Republic	3/93	Egypt	6/94	Cameroon	9/92
El Salvador	9/91	Jamaica	9/95	Congo	5/92
Guatemala	3/93[2]	Jordan	2/94	Côte d'Ivoire	9/92
Morocco	12/92	Peru	3/96	Ecuador	12/92
		Poland	3/94	Nigeria	3/92
				Philippines	3/93
Other middle-income countries					
Chile	12/88	Argentina	3/95	Bulgaria	4/93
Costa Rica	6/93[2]	Brazil	8/93	Gabon	12/92
Mexico	5/92	Russian Federation	12/93		
Panama	3/92				
Romania	12/83				
Trinidad and Tobago	3/91				
Turkey	6/83				
Yugoslavia	6/89				

Sources: Debt-rescheduling agreements; and IMF staff estimates.

[1] Asterisk (*) denotes rescheduling on enhanced concessional terms.

[2] Rescheduling of arrears only.

[3] Defined here as countries that obtained longer maturities in Paris Club reschedulings.

Table A7. Evolution of Paris Club Rescheduling Terms

	Standard	Lower Middle-Income Countries	Low-Income Countries					
			Toronto terms[1,2]			Enhanced concessions[2,3]		
			Option			Option		
			DR	DSR	LM	DR	DSR	LM
Implemented	. . .	Sept. 1990	Oct. 1988–June 1991			December 1991		
Grace *(in years)*	5–6	Up to 8	8	8	14	6	—	16[4]
Maturity *(in years)*	10	15	14	14	25	23	23	25
Repayment schedule	Flat/ graduated	Flat	Flat	Flat	Flat	Graduated	Graduated	Flat
Interest rate[5]	Market	Market	Market	Reduced[6]	Market	Market	Reduced[7]	Market
Reduction in net present value *(in percent)*	—	—	33	20–30[6]	—	50	50	—
Provision for stock operation	No	No	No	No	No	Yes	Yes	Yes
Memorandum items ODA credits								
Grace *(in years)*	5–6	Up to 10	14	14	14	12	12	16[4]
Maturity *(in years)*	10	20	25	25	25	30	30	25

Sources: Debt-rescheduling agreements; and IMF staff estimates.

[1]A detailed description of the Toronto terms can be found in Michael G. Kuhn, with Jorge P. Guzman, *Multilateral Official Debt Rescheduling: Recent Experience*, World Economic and Financial Surveys (Washington: International Monetary Fund, November 1990), pp. 14–16.

[2]DR refers to the debt-reduction option, DSR to the debt-service reduction option, and LM denotes the nonconcessional option providing longer maturities. The enhanced concessions menu includes a third concessional option that is a variant of the DSR option.

[3]The menu has also been called "Enhanced Toronto terms," or, misleadingly, "Trinidad terms."

[4]Fourteen years before June 1992.

[5]Interest rates are based on market rates and are determined in the bilateral agreements implementing the Paris Club Agreed Minute.

[6]The DSR option is 3.5 percentage points below market rate or half of market rate if market rate is below 7 percent. The degree of net present value reduction therefore varies.

[7]Reduced to achieve a 50 percent net present value reduction.

Table A8. OECD Country Classification[1]

Least-Developed Countries	Other Low-Income Countries	Lower Middle-Income Countries	Upper Middle-Income Countries and Regions
*Afghanistan	*Angola	Algeria	Antigua and Barbuda
*Bangladesh	*Bolivia	Anguilla	Argentina
*Benin	**China	Belize	Aruba
*Bhutan	**Côte d'Ivoire	Cameroon	Bahamas
Botswana	**Egypt	Chile	Bahrain
*Burkina Faso	*Ghana	Colombia	Barbados
*Burundi	*Guyana	Congo	Bermuda
*Cape Verde	*Honduras	Cook Islands	Brazil
*Central African Republic	**India	Costa Rica	Cayman Islands
*Chad	Indonesia	Cuba	Cyprus
*Comoros	*Kenya	**Dominica	Gabon
*Djibouti	*Nicaragua	Dominican Republic	Greece
*Equatorial Guinea	**Nigeria	Ecuador	Hong Kong
*Ethiopia	**Pakistan	El Salvador	Iraq
*Gambia	**Philippines	Fiji	Israel
*Guinea	*Senegal	Guatemala	Korea, Republic of
*Guinea-Bissau	*Sri Lanka	**Grenada	Lebanon
*Haiti	*Viet Nam	Guyana	Mexico
*Kampuchea, Democratic	**Zimbabwe	Iran, Islamic Rep. of	Montserrat
*Kiribati		Jamaica	Netherlands Antilles
*Laos		Jordan	Niue
*Lesotho		Malaysia	Oman
*Liberia		Mauritius	Seychelles
*Madagascar		Morocco	Singapore
*Malawi		Nauru	St. Kitts and Nevis
*Mali		Panama	Suriname
*Mauritania		Papua New Guinea	Taiwan Province of China
*Mozambique		Paraguay	Trinidad and Tobago
*Myanmar		Peru	Uruguay
*Nepal		St. Lucia	Virgin Islands
*Niger		St. Vincent and the	Yugoslavia, former
*Rwanda		Grenadines	Socialist Federal
*Sao Tome and Principe		Swaziland	Republic of
*Sierra Leone		Syrian Arab Republic	
*Solomon Islands		Thailand	
*Somalia		Tokelau	
*Sudan		*Tonga	
*Tanzania		Tunisia	
*Togo		Turkey	
Tuvalu		Turks and Caicos Islands	
*Uganda			
*Vanuatu			
*Western Samoa			
*Yemen			
*Zaïre			
*Zambia			

[1]Countries listed in country pages of *Geographical Distribution of Financial Flows to Developing Countries* of OECD only. Categorized in accordance with the following OECD definition (and differs somewhat from the definition used to categorize countries in Section III of this paper).

Least-developed countries include those on the UN list of least-developed countries, which include some countries with a per capita GNP in 1991 of over $765; other low-income countries include those whose per capita GNP in 1991 was below approximately $765 excluding least-developed countries; lower middle-income countries include those with a per capita GNP in 1991 between $765 and $2,555; and upper middle-income countries include those with a per capita GNP in 1991 exceeding $2,555.

An * indicates countries that receive IDA resources only; ** indicate countries that receive a blend of IDA and IBRD resources in accordance with the World Bank guideline based on a 1991 per capita GNP. Rescheduling countries are in italics.

As of January 1, 1993, five countries of the former Soviet Union have been added to the list (Kazakhstan, Kyrgyz Republic, Tajikistan, Turkmenistan, and Uzbekistan) but are not included in the table, which reflects classifications by the end of 1992.

Table A9. Overview of Reschedulings of Official Bilateral Debt, 1976–June 1993

Debtor Countries[1]	Date of Agreement	Amount Consoli-dated[2]	Consolidation Period[3]	Terms[4,5]	
				Grace	Maturity
			(In months)	*(In years)*	
Angola I	7/89	446	15	6.0	9.5
Argentina I	1/85	2,040	12	5.0	9.5
Argentina II	5/87	1,260	14	4.9	9.5
Argentina III	12/89	2,450	15	5.8	9.3
Argentina IV	9/91	1,476	9	6.2	9.7
Argentina V	7/92	2,701	33	1.1	13.6
Benin I	6/89	193	13	Toronto terms	
Benin II	12/91	129	19	Enhanced concessions	
Benin III	6/93	25	29	Enhanced concessions	
Bolivia I	7/86	449	12	5.0	9.5
Bolivia II	11/88	226	15	5.9	9.3
Bolivia III	3/90	300	24	Toronto terms	
Bolivia IV	1/92	65	18	Enhanced concessions	
Brazil I	11/83	2,337	17	4.0	7.5
Brazil II	1/87	4,178	30	3.0	5.5
Brazil III	7/88	4,992	20	5.0	9.5
Brazil IV	2/92	10,500	20	1.8	13.3
Bulgaria I	4/91	640	12	6.5	10.0
Bulgaria II	12/92	251	5	6.3	9.8
Burkina Faso I	3/91	63	15	Toronto terms	
Burkina Faso II	5/93	36	33	Enhanced concessions	
Cameroon I	5/89	535	12	6.0	9.5
Cameroon II	1/92	1,080	9	8.2	14.5
Central African Republic I	6/81	72	12	4.0	8.5
Central African Republic II	7/83	13	12	5.0	9.5
Central African Republic III	11/85	14	18	4.8	9.3
Central African Republic IV	12/88	28	18	Toronto terms	
Central African Republic V	6/90	4	12	Toronto terms	
Chad I	10/89[6]	38	15	Toronto terms	
Chile I	7/85	146	18	2.8	6.3
Chile II	4/87	157	21	2.6	6.1
Congo I	7/86	756	20	3.7	9.1
Congo II	9/90	1,052	21	5.8	14.3
Costa Rica I	1/83	136	18	3.8	8.3
Costa Rica II	4/85	166	15	4.9	9.4
Costa Rica III	5/89	182	14	4.9	9.4
Costa Rica IV	7/91	139	9	5.0	9.5
Costa Rica V	6/93	58	—	2.0	6.5
Côte d'Ivoire I	5/84	230	13	4.0	8.5
Côte d'Ivoire II	6/85	213	12	4.0	8.5
Côte d'Ivoire III	6/86	370	36	4.1	8.6
Côte d'Ivoire IV	12/87	567	16	5.8	9.3
Côte d'Ivoire V	12/89	934	16	7.8	13.3
Côte d'Ivoire VI	11/91	806	12	8.0	14.5
Dominican Republic I	5/85	290	15	4.9	9.4
Dominican Republic II	11/91	850	18	7.8	14.3
Ecuador I	7/83	142	12	3.0	7.5
Ecuador II	4/85	450	36	3.0	7.5
Ecuador III	1/88	438	14	4.9	9.4
Ecuador IV	10/89	397	14	5.9	9.4
Ecuador V	1/92	339	12	8.0	15.0
Egypt I	5/87	6,350	18	4.7	9.2
Egypt II	5/91	27,864[7]	. . .	2.5	35.0
El Salvador I	9/90	135	13	8.0	14.5

61

Table A9. *(continued)*

Debtor Countries[1]	Date of Agreement	Amount Consoli-dated[2]	Consolidation Period[3]	Terms[4,5]	
				Grace	Maturity
			(In months)	*(In years)*	
Equatorial Guinea I	7/85	38	18	4.5	9.0
Equatorial Guinea II	3/89[6]	10	—	Toronto terms	
Equatorial Guinea III	4/92[6]	32	12	Enhanced concessions	
Ethiopia I	12/92	441	35	Enhanced concessions	
Gabon I	6/78	63	—	—	—
Gabon II	1/87	387	15	3.9	9.4
Gabon III	3/88	326	12	5.0	9.5
Gabon IV	9/89	545	16	4.0	10.0
Gabon V	10/91	498	15	5.0	10.0
Gambia, The I	9/86	17	12	5.0	9.5
Guatemala I	3/93	440	—	8.0	14.5
Guinea I	4/86	196	14	4.9	9.4
Guinea II	4/89	123	12	Toronto terms	
Guinea III	11/92	203	—	Enhanced concessions	
Guinea-Bissau I	10/87	25	18	9.7	19.2
Guinea-Bissau II	10/89	21	15	Toronto terms	
Guyana I	5/89	195	14	9.9	19.4
Guyana II	9/90	123	35	Toronto terms	
Guyana III	5/93	39	17	Enhanced concessions	
Honduras I	9/90	280	18	8.1	14.6
Honduras II	10/92	180	34	Enhanced concessions	
Jamaica I	7/84	105	15	3.9	8.4
Jamaica II	7/85	62	12	4.0	9.5
Jamaica III	3/87	124	15	4.9	9.4
Jamaica IV	10/88	147	18	4.7	9.2
Jamaica V	4/90	179	18	4.8	9.3
Jamaica VI	7/91	127	13	6.0	14.5
Jamaica VII	1/93	291	36	5.0	13.5
Jordan I	7/89	587	18	4.8	9.3
Jordan II	2/92	603	18	7.7	14.3
Liberia I	12/80	35	18	3.3	7.8
Liberia II	12/81	25	18	4.1	8.6
Liberia III	12/83	17	12	4.0	8.5
Liberia IV	12/84	17	12	5.0	9.5
Madagascar I	4/81	140	18	3.8	8.3
Madagascar II	7/82	107	12	3.8	8.3
Madagascar III	3/84	89	18	4.8	10.3
Madagascar IV	5/85	128	15	4.9	10.4
Madagascar V	10/86	212	24	4.6	9.1
Madagascar VI	10/88	254	21	Toronto terms	
Madagascar VII	7/90	139	13	Toronto terms	
Malawi I	9/82	25	12	3.5	8.0
Malawi II	10/83	26	12	3.5	8.0
Malawi III	4/88	27	14	9.9	19.4
Mali I	10/88	63	16	Toronto terms	
Mali II	11/89	44	26	Toronto terms	
Mali III	10/92	20	35	Enhanced concessions	
Mauritania I	4/85	68	15	3.8	8.3
Mauritania II	5/86	27	12	4.0	8.5
Mauritania III	6/87	90	14	4.9	14.4
Mauritania IV	6/89	52	12	Toronto terms	
Mauritania V	1/93	218	24	Enhanced concessions	
Mexico I	6/83	1,199	6	3.0	5.5
Mexico II	9/86	1,912	18	4.0	8.5
Mexico III	5/89	2,400	36	6.1	9.6

Table A9. *(continued)*

Debtor Countries[1]	Date of Agreement	Amount Consolidated[2]	Consolidation Period[3]	Terms[4,5] Grace	Maturity
			(In months)	*(In years)*	
Morocco I	10/83	1,152	16	3.8	7.3
Morocco II	9/85	1,124	18	3.8	8.3
Morocco III	3/87	1,008	16	4.7	9.2
Morocco IV	10/88	969	18	4.7	9.2
Morocco V	9/90	1,390	7	7.9	14.4
Morocco VI	2/92	1,303	11	8.1	14.5
Mozambique I	10/84	283	12	5.0	10.5
Mozambique II	6/87	361	19	9.7	19.3
Mozambique III	6/90	719	30	Toronto terms	
Mozambique IV	3/93	440	24	Enhanced concessions	
Nicaragua I	12/91	355	15	Enhanced concessions	
Niger I	11/83	36	12	4.5	8.5
Niger II	11/84	26	14	4.9	9.4
Niger III	11/85	38	12	5.1	9.5
Niger IV	11/86	34	12	5.0	9.5
Niger V	4/88	37	13	10.0	19.5
Niger VI	12/88	48	12	Toronto terms	
Niger VII	9/90	116	28	Toronto terms	
Nigeria I	12/86	6,251	15	4.9	9.4
Nigeria II	3/89	5,600	16	4.8	9.3
Nigeria III	1/91	3,300	15	7.9	14.3
Panama I	9/85	19	16	2.8	7.3
Panama II	11/90	200	17	4.8	9.3
Peru I	11/78	420	12	2.0	6.5
Peru II	7/83	466	12	3.0	7.5
Peru III	6/84	704	15	4.9	8.4
Peru IV	9/91	5,910	15	7.9	14.5
Peru V	5/93	1,527	39	6.9	13.4
Philippines I	12/84	757	18	4.8	9.3
Philippines II	1/87	862	18	4.7	9.2
Philippines III	5/89	1,850	25	5.5	9.0
Philippines IV	6/91	1,096	14	7.9	14.4
Poland I	4/81	2,110	8	4.0	7.5
Poland II	7/85	10,930	36	5.0	10.5
Poland III	11/85	1,400	12	5.0	9.5
Poland IV	10/87	9,027	12	4.5	9.0
Poland V	2/90	10,400	15	8.3	13.8
Poland VI	4/91	29,871[8]	...	6.5	18.0
Romania I	7/82	234	12	3.0	6.0
Romania II	5/83	736	12	3.0	6.0
Russian Federation I	4/93	14,363	12	5.0	9.5
Senegal I	10/81	75	12	4.0	8.5
Senegal II	11/82	74	12	4.3	8.8
Senegal III	12/83	72	12	4.0	8.5
Senegal IV	1/85	122	18	3.8	8.3
Senegal V	11/86	65	16	4.8	9.3
Senegal VI	11/87	79	12	6.0	15.5
Senegal VII	1/89	143	14	Toronto terms	
Senegal VIII	2/90	107	12	Toronto terms	
Senegal IX	6/91	114	12	Toronto terms	
Sierra Leone I	9/77	39	24	1.5	8.5
Sierra Leone II	2/80	37	16	4.2	9.7
Sierra Leone III	2/84	25	12	5.0	10.0
Sierra Leone IV	11/86	86	16	4.8	9.2
Sierra Leone V	11/92	164	16	Enhanced concessions	
Somalia I	3/85	127	12	5.0	9.5
Somalia II	7/87	153	24	9.5	19.0

Table A9. *(concluded)*

Debtor Countries[1]	Date of Agreement	Amount Consolidated[2]	Consolidation Period[3]	Terms[4,5] Grace	Terms[4,5] Maturity
			(In months)	*(In years)*	
Sudan I	11/79	487	21	3.0	9.5
Sudan II	3/82	203	18	4.5	9.5
Sudan III	2/83	518	12	5.5	15.0
Sudan IV	5/84	249	12	6.0	15.5
Tanzania I	9/86	1,046	12	5.0	9.5
Tanzania II	12/88	377	6	Toronto terms	
Tanzania III	3/90	199	12	Toronto terms	
Tanzania IV	1/92	691	30	Enhanced concessions	
Togo I	6/79	260	21	2.8	8.3
Togo II	2/81	232	24	4.0	8.5
Togo III	4/83	300	12	5.0	9.5
Togo IV	6/84	75	16	4.8	9.3
Togo V	6/85	27	12	5.0	10.5
Togo VI	3/88	139	15	7.9	15.3
Togo VII	6/89	76	14	Toronto terms	
Togo VIII	7/90	88	24	Toronto terms	
Togo IX	6/92	52	24	Enhanced concessions	
Trinidad and Tobago I	1/89	209	14	4.9	9.4
Trinidad and Tobago II	4/90	110	13	5.0	9.5
Turkey I	5/78	1,300	13	2.0	6.5
Turkey II	7/79	1,200	12	3.0	7.5
Turkey III	7/80	3,000	36	4.5	9.0
Uganda I	11/81	30	12	4.5	9.0
Uganda II	12/82	19	12	6.5	8.0
Uganda III	6/87	170	12	6.0	14.5
Uganda IV	1/89	89	18	Toronto terms	
Uganda V	6/92	39	17	Enhanced concessions	
Yugoslavia[9]	5/84	500	12	4.0	6.5
Yugoslavia II[9]	5/85	812	17	3.8	8.3
Yugoslavia III[9]	5/86	901	23	3.9	9.4
Yugoslavia IV[9]	7/88	1,291	15	5.9	9.4
Zaïre I	6/76	270	18	1.0	7.5
Zaïre II	7/77	170	12	3.0	8.5
Zaïre III	12/77	40	6	3.0	9.0
Zaïre IV	12/79	1,040	18	3.5	9.0
Zaïre V	7/81	500	12	4.0	9.5
Zaïre VI	12/83	1,497	12	5.0	10.5
Zaïre VII	9/85	408	15	4.9	9.4
Zaïre VIII	5/86	429	12	4.0	9.5
Zaïre IX	5/87	671	13	6.0	14.5
Zaïre X	6/89	1,530	13	Toronto terms	
Zambia I	5/83	375	12	5.0	9.5
Zambia II	7/84	253	12	5.0	9.5
Zambia III	3/86	371	12	5.0	9.5
Zambia IV	7/90	963	18	Toronto terms	
Zambia V	7/92	917	33	Enhanced concessions	

Sources: Debt-rescheduling agreements; and IMF staff estimates.

[1]Roman numerals indicate, for each country, the number of debt reschedulings since 1976.

[2]In millions of U.S. dollars. Includes debt service formally rescheduled as well as postponed maturities.

[3]In a number of cases consolidation period was extended.

[4]Terms for current maturities due on medium- and long-term debt covered by the rescheduling agreement and not rescheduled previously.

[5]In this paper, grace and maturity of rescheduled current maturities are counted from the end of the consolidation period. In cases of multiyear rescheduling, the effective average repayment period can be longer. For repayment schedules under Toronto terms and enhanced concessions, see Table A7.

[6]Date of informal meeting of creditors on the terms to be applied in the bilateral reschedulings.

[7]Total value of debt restructured, including the cancellation of military debt by the United States.

[8]Total value of debt restructured.

[9]Former Socialist Federal Republic of Yugoslavia.

Table A10. Reschedulings of Official Bilateral Debt, 1991–June 1993[1]

Debtor Countries[2]	Date of Agreement	Amount Consoli- dated[3]	Consolidation Period	Terms[4,5] Grace	Maturity
			(In months)	*(In years)*	
1991					
Nigeria III	January 18	3,300	15	7.9	14.3
Burkina Faso I	March 15	63	15	Toronto terms	
Bulgaria I	April 17	640	12	6.5	10.0
Poland VI	April 21	29,871[6]	...	6.5	18.0
Egypt II	May 25	27,864[6]	...	4.5	32.5
Philippines IV	June 20	1,096	14	7.9	14.4
Senegal IX	June 21	114	12	Toronto terms	
Costa Rica IV	July 16	139	9	5.0	9.5
Jamaica VI	July 19	127	13	6.0	14.5
Peru IV	September 17	5,910	15	7.9	14.5
Argentina IV	September 19	1,476	9	6.2	9.7
Gabon V	October 24	498	15	5.0	10.0
Côte d'Ivoire VI	November 20	806	12	8.0	14.5
Dominican Republic II	November 22	850	18	7.8	14.3
Nicaragua I	December 17	355	15	Enhanced concessions	
Benin II	December 18	129	19	Enhanced concessions	
1992					
Ecuador V	January 20	339	12	8.0	15.0
Tanzania IV	January 21	691	30	Enhanced concessions	
Cameroon II	January 23	1,080	9	8.2	14.6
Bolivia IV	January 24	65	18	Enhanced concessions	
Brazil IV	February 26	10,500	20	1.8	13.3
Morocco VI	February 27	1,303	11	8.1	14.5
Jordan II	February 28	603	18	7.7	14.3
Equatorial Guinea III	April 2	32	12	Enhanced concessions	
Uganda V	June 17	39	17	Enhanced concessions	
Togo IX	June 19	52	24	Enhanced concessions	
Argentina V	July 22	2,701	33	1.1	13.6
Zambia V	July 23	917	33	Enhanced concessions	
Honduras II	October 26	180	34	Enhanced concessions	
Mali III	October 29	20	35	Enhanced concessions	
Guinea III	November 18	203	—	Enhanced concessions	
Sierra Leone V	November 20	164	16	Enhanced concessions	
Bulgaria II	December 14	251	5	6.3	9.8
Ethiopia I	December 16	441	35	Enhanced concessions	
1993					
Jamaica VII	January 25	291	36	5.0	13.5
Mauritania V	January 26	218	24	Enhanced concessions	
Mozambique IV	March 23	440	24	Enhanced concessions	
Guatemala I	March 25	440	—	8.0	14.5
Russian Federation I	April 2	14,363	12	5.0	9.5
Peru V	May 4	1,527	39	6.9	13.4
Guyana III	May 6	39	17	Enhanced concessions	
Burkina Faso II	May 7	36	33	Enhanced concessions	
Benin III	June 21	25	29	Enhanced concessions	
Costa Rica V	June 22	58	—	2.0	6.5

Sources: Debt-rescheduling agreements; and IMF staff estimates.

[1]A complete listing is provided in Table A9.

[2]Roman numerals indicate, for each country, the number of debt reschedulings since 1976.

[3]In millions of U.S. dollars. Includes debt service formally rescheduled, as well as postponed maturities.

[4]Terms for current maturities due on medium- and long-term debt covered by the rescheduling agreement.

[5]In this paper, grace and maturities are counted from the end of the consolidation period. For multiyear rescheduling, the effective average repayment period can be longer. For repayment schedules under Toronto terms and enhanced concessions, see Table A7.

[6]Total value of debt stock restructured.

Table A11. Selected Debt-Restructuring Agreements Involving Official Bilateral Creditors Not Participating in the Paris Club, 1987–93[1]

Creditors	Debtors	Date of Agreement	Amount (In millions of U.S. dollars)		Coverage	Terms	Other
			Total	Of which: Arrears			
Latin American and Caribbean							
1. Argentina	Bolivia	9/87	689	226	D, including A	Repayment over 25 years with 15 years' grace at fixed 8 percent interest.	Agreement inoperative following accumulation of arrears on current payments by Argentina.
	Bolivia	8/89	813	83	D, including A; LAIA clearing account (net)	Cancellation of credits against $314 million of debts (including arrears) owed to Bolivia.	
2. Brazil	Angola	1990	...	...	A as of 12/89 on NPRD	Repayment over 8 years, with 1 year's grace.	Additional financing of $20 million short term, $60 million medium-term trade, and $100 million project.
	Bolivia	2/90	395	128	(a) P+I in 1990–96	(a) Options: (1) rescheuled as under Paris Club rescheduling; (2) 50 percent covered by grant, remaining on original schedule; (3) buy-back using Brazilian commercial debt at variable discount.	Option (3) was chosen.
					(b) A as of 12/89	(b) Buy-back using Brazilian commercial debt at full discount.	
	Costa Rica	6/88	26	26	D, including A	Two tranches: (1) repayment over 7 years, with 3 years' grace; (2) repayment over 9 years, with 5 years' grace. Interest at LIBOR + 1.25 percent.	
	Dominican Republic	1993	11	...	D, including A	Buy-back at a 68 percent discount.	
	Guyana	10/89	24	...	Dt, including At	Medium- and long-term (short-term) debt to be repaid over 18 (10) years, with 5.5 years' grace at LIBOR + 13/16 percent.	
	Jordan	4/93	42	...	D, including A	Agreement that Jordan should purchase Brazilian debt to commercial banks in the secondary market at a discount and exchange it for Jordan's debt to Brazil at par.	Purchases of Brazilian debt not yet made.
	Mozambique	1992	325	...	A	Repayment over 15 years with rising schedule of payments. Interest of LIBOR + 1 percent. Option to purchase Brazilian debt to commercial banks in the secondary market at a discount and exchange at par.	Figure is Mozambique's total debt to Brazil. Not known whether all of this or just arrears was rescheduled.

Country	Date			Description	Terms	Remarks
Paraguay	4/89	490	...	D, including A	Options: (1) repayment over 20 years, with 8 years' grace and spread $^{13}/_{16}$ over LIBOR; (2) buy-back using Brazilian commercial debt at variable discount.	Buy-back option was chosen in 1990.
Costa Rica	2/91	70	...	D, including A	Repayment over 14 years on a graduated schedule, with 1 year's grace, at LIBOR.	
	6/91	35	...	Credits disbursed in 1990 for buying back bank debt of Costa Rica.	Repayment over 2 years, with 1 year's grace.	
Dominican Republic	1987	109	...	Short-term obligations of the Central Bank of the Dominican Republic.	Repayment over 6 years.	
	3/88	76	45	Certain debts owed to Venezuelan Investment Fund (VIF), Central Government and Central Bank.	...	
	3/89	9	4	Certain debts owed to VIF.	Repayment over 7 years, with 4 years' grace.	
	8/90	234	...	Amounts rescheduled in 1987 (including A, $142 million) and ALADI ($92 million).	Options: (1) debt conversions; (2) certain amounts payable over 1 year, but most over 10 years, with 3 years' grace.	
3. Venezuela	1992	265	...	Debt rescheduled in 1990 and arrears on this debt.	Buy-back at a 68 percent discount.	
Guyana	1991	14	14	A	Rescheduling of arrears to VIF with 10-year maturities 2 years' grace and an interest rate of 6 percent.	
Honduras	1991	42	36	A, P+I through end-1992	$30 million rescheduled to be paid over 10-year period; rest refinanced through oil financing arrangement.	
Jamaica	1987	109	...	A, 1987–89 P+I	...	
	12/89	102	...	P, including A	Refinancing over 7 years with new disbursements under oil financing arrangement.	
Nicaragua	1991	300	...	D, including A (95 percent of total debt)	40-year bullet with principal guarantee (zero coupon bond); interest payments to begin after 7 years and to depend on export performance.	Zero coupon bonds to be paid for from the reactivation of oil financing arrangement.

Table A11. (continued)

Creditors	Debtors	Date of Agreement	Amount		Coverage	Terms	Other
			Total	Of which: Arrears			
			(In millions of U.S. dollars)				
4. Mexico	Costa Rica	6/88	153	83	D, including A	Repayment over 14 years on a graduated schedule, with 4 years' grace, at LIBOR.	Semi-annual interest and principal may be paid with Mexican debt purchased in secondary markets (discounts shared).
		6/91	35	–	1990 loan used for buying back bank debt of Costa Rica	Repayment over 2 years, with 1 year's grace.	
	Cuba	2/90	350	...	D, including A	Debts repaid with purchase of Cuban products; also, converted into equity in joint ventures in tourism, industry, and agriculture.	
	Dominican Republic	12/91	163	...	D, including A	Buy-back at 32.5 percent of face value, which is close to price of Dominican Republic's commercial bank debt.	
	El Salvador	1990	48	...	D, including A	Buy-back using commercial debt of Mexico purchased in secondary markets (shared discounts).	
	Honduras	6/90	42	35	D, including A	Repayment over 6 years with 2 years' grace, except for $3 million that was to be paid within 6 months.	
		1/91	...	...	All D, including A	28.5 year bullet with principal guarantee (zero coupon bond); interest rate would be 6.5 percent or 3 month LIBOR + $^{13}/_{16}$ percent, whichever is lower in first 5 years, and LIBOR + $^{13}/_{16}$ percent thereafter.	Following agreement Mexico is to open line of credit for $50 million.
	Nicaragua	1/92	55	...	...	...	
		1991	1,084	...	D, including A (95 percent of total debt)	40-year bullet with principal guarantee (zero coupon bond); interest payments to begin after 7 years and to depend on export performance.	Zero coupon bonds to be paid for from the reactivation of oil financing arrangement.
5. Trinidad and Tobago	Guyana	1989	402	...	D, including A at end of 1989, 1989–91 P+I	Repayment over 20 years with 10 (1.5) years' grace in the case of principal (interest). Late interest canceled.	
6. Barbados and Other Caribbean Trade Facility Members	Guyana	1990	146	146	A at end of 1989	Repayment over with 10 (0.5) years' grace in the case of principal (interest). Interest on interest arrears were waived.	

Arab countries

1. Arab African Bank	Egypt	1990	279	...	D, including A	Canceled
2. GODE	Egypt	1990	2,592	...	D, including A	Canceled
3. Iraq	Viet Nam	5/90	317	...	D, including A	Repayment over 10 years, with 4 years' grace, at 5 percent interest.
4. Libya	Uganda	2/89	14	14	A	Repayment in 5 years, with 2 years' grace.
	Viet Nam	6/90	40	...	A	Repayment over 7 years, at 2½ percent interest.
5. Kuwait	Egypt	1990	1,895	...	D, including A	Canceled
6. Qatar	Egypt	1990	93	...	D, including A	Canceled
7. Saudi Arabia	Uganda	11/88	13	13	A	Repayment in 10 years, with 2 years' grace.
	Countries affected by Gulf crisis	1990	5,700[2]	...	D, including A	Canceled
	Of which: Egypt		1,138	...	D, including A	Canceled
	Morocco		2,753	...	D, including A	Canceled
	Low-income African countries[3]	1991	307[2]	...	D, including A	Canceled all official credits.
	Burkina Faso	9/91	2	...	D, including A	Rescheduled over 5½ years with 1 year's grace.
	Mauritania	3/93	26	26	A	Rescheduled over 6 years with lower payments for the first 2 years and with zero interest.
8. United Arab Emirates	Egypt	1990	304	...	D, including A	Canceled

Eastern Europe and former Soviet Union

1. German Democratic Republic, former	Nicaragua	1988	800	...	...	...
2. U.S.S.R., former	Peru	3/87	20	...	Payments to begin in 1988 ($3 million).	To be paid with exports.
	Angola	12/87	1,000	...	A, P+I to 12/90	Repayment over 8.5 years, with 3.5 years' grace, at 3 percent interest.
	Angola	7/89	1,205	786	A at end of 1989, P+I through end of 1990	Repayment over 10 years, with 7 years' grace, at 3 percent interest. Late interest canceled at 5 percent interest. Remaining debt ($19 million) to be negotiated.
	Nicaragua	1988	300–400	...	D, including A	To be paid in full in 1991.
	Nigeria	12/90	870	870	A, 1989–90 P+I	Repayment over 6 years, with ½ year's grace.

Table A11. *(concluded)*

Creditors	Debtors	Date of Agreement	Amount Total	Amount Of which: Arrears	Coverage	Terms	Other
			(In millions of U.S. dollars)				
	Peru	1988	Rub 570	…	D, including A	Repayment over more than 10 years, at 3 percent interest; payments to rise gradually from Rub 30 million/year in 1988–91 to Rub 70 million after 1991.	
3. Russian Federation	Jordan	1992	614	…	D, including A	Buy-back	Payment in cash in 1992 and in exports in 1993.
	Tanzania	1/93	635	…	D, including A	Payment of $22 million in debt service in 1993.	No agreements on treatment of stock of debt, or debt service beyond 1993.
Other countries							
1. Algeria	Viet Nam	8/90	216	…	D, including A	Repayment over 10–15 years, at 2 percent interest.	
	Burkina Faso	3/92	8	…	D, including A	Repayment over 12 years, with 4 years' grace and zero interest.	
2. Korea	Uganda	5/91	…	…	…	…	
3. China	Guinea	1991	55	55	A	Rescheduling on concessional terms.	
	Guyana	6/92	18	…	D	Postponement of repayment for 5 years.	Interest free loan.
4. Côte d'Ivoire	Burkina Faso	12/91	100	…	D, including A	Repayment on 15 years with 2 years' grace and zero interest.	
5. India	Viet Nam	1/89	8	…	D, including A	Repayment over 9 years, with 2 years' grace, at 6.5 percent interest.	

Source: Information provided by debtors.

[1]Key: A = arrears on D; ALADI = Associación Latinoamericana de Integración (LAIA); At = arrears on Dt; D = medium- and long-term debt; Dt = debt of all maturities; I = interest, medium- and long-term debt; GODE = Gulf Organization for the Development of Egypt; LAIA = Latin American Integration Association (ALADI); NPRD = not previously rescheduled debt; P = principal, medium- and long-term debt.

[2]Creditor information.

[3]Includes Cameroon, the Comoros, Djibouti, Guinea, Niger, Senegal, Somalia, and Uganda.

Table A12. Official Bilateral Debt Cancellations, 1985–91[1]

(In millions of U.S. dollars)

Debtor country	1985	1986	1987	1988	1989	1990	1991	Total 1985–91
Bangladesh	50		28				260	338
Belize						9		9
Benin[2,3]			*	2	29	78	14	123
Bolivia[2,3]	*			1	754	107	401	1,263
Botswana			5					5
Burkina Faso[2,3]			10		189	5	1	205
Burundi						106	3	109
Cameroon			96	18	3		2	119
Central African Republic[2]		*		1	4	133		138
Chad[2]					67	7		74
China			102					102
Colombia						2		2
Comoros					26	*	14	40
Congo			18		5			23
Costa Rica						*	1	1
Côte d'Ivoire		3	25					28
Cyprus	*							
Djibouti	2				25			27
Dominica						2		2
Dominican Republic	*							
Ecuador						1		1
Egypt		*	*		2,705	10,319		13,024
El Salvador			*					
Equatorial Guinea[2,3]						18		18
Ethiopia[3]		2				67		69
Ghana	83		*	17	50	102	104	357
Guatemala					*			
Guinea[2,3]	5	*			292	2	11	310
Guinea-Bissau[2]	*			2	*	1		4
Guyana[2,3]					2	31	177	210
Haiti	12		3				167	182
Honduras[3]							442	442
Iran, Islamic Rep. of					27			27
Jamaica						*	217	217
Jordan		10			15			25
Kenya		14	47	9	461	63	41	635
Lao, People's Democratic Rep. of				10			29	39
Lesotho		3				*		3
Liberia					*			
Madagascar[2]	1		18	*	305	240	3	557
Malawi						51	2	53
Maldives		*						
Mali[2,3]				29	6	2	1	38
Mauritania[2,3]			33		69	66		167
Mauritius					3			3
Morocco	1						2,742	2,743
Mozambique[2,3]						211	55	266
Myanmar	6			*			72	78
Nicaragua[3]							272	272
Niger[2]		8	11		254	*	26	299
Nigeria					32	*	14	46
Pakistan	*	1	7	2				10
Panama	4			*	*			5
Papua New Guinea				40				40
Paraguay					107			107
Peru	*							
Philippines			*	35				35

Table A12. *(concluded)*

Debtor country	1985	1986	1987	1988	1989	1990	1991	Total 1985–91
Poland						578	1	579
Rwanda					46			46
Senegal[2]		2			860	18	141	1,021
Sierra Leone[3]		4	1					5
Somalia	4	10	7					21
Sri Lanka		*				*		
St. Lucia						*		
St. Vincent and the Grenadines						1		1
Sudan	45	4	26	5				80
Swaziland			1					1
Tanzania[2,3]				1	1	5	4	11
Thailand				2				2
Togo[2,3]	9	7		4	154	18	2	195
Trinidad and Tobago						7		7
Tunisia	1		4		3	7	13	28
Uganda[2,3]	7		13	41	2	21	*	84
Yemen				3				3
Zaïre[2]	4	24	23	324	137	7		520
Zambia[2,3]	*	35			188	119	87	429
Zimbabwe						24	7	32
Total	235	125	513	512	6,826	12,702	5,054	25,967

Sources: World Bank Debtor Reporting System; and IMF staff estimates.

[1]Totals include amounts canceled under the provisions of Paris Club multilateral debt reschedulings on Toronto and enhanced concessional terms; totals may not add up due to rounding. Asterisk (*) denotes amounts of $0.5 million and less.

[2]Countries that obtained reschedulings on Toronto terms.

[3]Countries that obtained reschedulings on enhanced concessional terms.

Table A13. Official Bilateral Financial Flows from DAC Countries by Income Group of Countries, Gross Disbursements, 1986–91[1]

(In millions of U.S. dollars)

	1986	1987	1988	1989	1990	1991
Least-developed countries	6,270	7,396	8,431	7,885	8,506	8,582
Grants[2]	4,851	5,349	6,167	5,957	6,769	7,383
Official development assistance (ODA) loans[3]	1,050	1,370	1,506	1,128	1,175	715
Other official credits and loans[3,4]	369	677	757	801	562	484
Official export credits[5]	39	20	82	28	39	67
Others[6]	330	656	675	773	523	417
Memorandum item						
Other official flows[7]	262	364	378	259	269	300
Other low-income countries	16,611	19,110	22,341	25,222	26,595	30,555
Grants[2]	5,145	5,320	6,147	6,805	10,681	11,652
ODA loans[3]	4,253	4,578	6,016	6,009	6,078	11,695
Other official credits and loans[3,4]	7,213	9,212	10,179	12,407	9,836	7,208
Official export credits[5]	811	702	624	1,081	1,352	1,710
Others[6]	6,402	8,510	9,554	11,326	8,484	5,499
Memorandum item						
Other official flows[7]	2,077	3,647	6,845	4,304	5,355	4,851
Lower middle-income countries	6,984	7,391	8,112	9,353	10,768	11,350
Grants[2]	2,125	2,466	2,655	2,794	3,406	4,108
ODA loans[3]	1,549	1,967	2,048	2,120	3,078	3,498
Other official credits and loans[3,4]	3,310	2,959	3,409	4,438	4,284	3,744
Official export credits[5]	653	623	632	731	748	796
Others[6]	2,657	2,336	2,777	3,708	3,535	2,948
Memorandum item						
Other official flows[7]	1,928	1,225	1,562	1,662	1,947	2,519
Upper middle-income countries	14,256	17,819	14,561	22,594	22,823	21,614
Grants[2]	3,137	2,757	2,831	2,785	3,378	4,023
ODA loans[3]	938	1,245	781	984	1,536	2,103
Other official credits and loans[3,4]	10,182	13,816	10,948	18,824	17,909	15,489
Official export credits[5]	1,620	1,453	1,078	1,664	2,755	2,848
Others[6]	8,562	12,364	9,870	17,161	15,154	12,641
Memorandum item						
Other official flows[7]	3,472	5,993	3,425	4,564	7,333	6,108
Total (including unallocated)	50,973	60,399	63,804	74,255	78,535	85,202
(Percent change over previous year)	. . .	19	6	16	6	9
ODA	27,849	31,478	34,863	35,861	43,808	54,065
(Percent change over previous year)	. . .	13	11	3	22	23
Grants[2]	19,852	21,958	24,381	25,480	31,789	35,933
Loans[3]	7,997	9,520	10,482	10,381	12,019	18,132
Other official credits and loans[3,4]	23,124	28,921	28,941	38,394	34,728	31,137
Official export credits[5]	3,125	2,831	2,470	3,622	5,106	5,551
Others[6]	19,999	26,090	26,471	34,772	29,622	25,586
Memorandum item						
Other official flows[7]	8,315	11,799	12,719	11,238	15,581	14,855
Total flows to low-income countries	22,881	26,506	30,772	33,107	35,101	39,137
Total flows to middle-income countries	21,240	25,210	22,673	31,947	33,591	32,964

Sources: OECD, *Geographical Distribution of Financial Flows to Developing Countries*; and data provided by the OECD.

Note: DAC denotes the Development Assistance Committee of the OECD.

[1]Categorized according to unchanged income group criteria.

[2]Include debt forgiveness, estimated to have totaled $1.4 billion in 1990 and $1.9 billion in 1991.

[3]Including debt reorganization; for example, in 1991 total ODA loans to other low-income countries include a large rescheduling of Egypt's debt.

[4]Contractual lending (defined as bilateral ODA and other official loans plus officially guaranteed private export credits) less bilateral ODA loans.

[5]Direct export credits from official sources.

[6]Contractual lending (see footnote 4 above) less bilateral ODA loans and official exports credits; that is, includes officially guaranteed and insured export credits and untied non-ODA official loans.

[7]Includes official export credits, untied non-ODA official loans, official sector equity and portfolio investment, and debt reorganization undertaken by the official sector on nonconcessional terms.

Table A14. Lending Terms of Major Multilateral Financial Institutions

Institutions	Interest Rate	Commitment Fee	Grace Period	Maturity
	(In percent)		*(In years)*	*(In years)*
African Development Bank	Variable	1.00	5	20
African Development Fund	0.75[1]		10	20
Asian Development Bank	Variable	0.75	3–6	10–30
Asian Development Fund	1–3[2]		10	35/40
Inter-American Development Bank				
Ordinary capital	Variable	0.75	6½[3]	15/20/25
Fund for special operations	1–4	0.50	5–10	25–40
World Bank				
International Bank for Reconstruction and Development	Variable	0.75	3–5	15/17/20
International Development Assistance	0.75[1]	0.50	10	35/40
Memorandum item				
International Monetary Fund (type of arrangement)				
Stand-by	Variable		3	5
EFF/STF	Variable		4½	10
SAF/ESAF	0.5		5½	10

Sources: Annual Reports and information obtained directly from the AfDB, AsDB, IDB, and various IMF and World Bank documents.

Note: EFF = extended Fund facility; STF = systemic transformation facility; SAF = structural adjustment facility; ESAF ≠ enhanced structural adjustment facility. This table summarizes the principal terms of key lending programs of the major multilateral financial institutions. These terms are indicative. Actual terms are determined on the basis of principles stipulated in the charter of each institution, and can vary depending on the stage of development of the country and on the nature of the project. Lending terms of multilateral development banks apply both to project and program loans. Interest rates are variable and are based on the cost of funding plus a margin determined on the basis of a targeted net income. Concessional resources are generally provided through a special "soft window" to qualifying countries, and concessional interest rates reflect the impact of subsidies provided through internal and external funding mechanisms. Commitment fees apply to undisbursed amounts. Grace period and maturity are longer the lower the income level of a member country.

[1]Service charge.
[2]Service fee of 0.75 percent included.
[3]Average.

Table A15. Official Bilateral Financial Flows from DAC Countries by Region, Gross Disbursements, 1986–91

(In millions of U.S. dollars)

	1986	1987	1988	1989	1990	1991
Sub-Saharan Africa	9,524	11,324	13,333	14,204	16,223	13,984
Grants[1]	5,445	5,901	7,082	7,128	10,306	9,469
Official development assistance (ODA) loans[2]	1,499	2,011	2,217	2,150	2,588	1,934
Other official credits and loans[2,3]	2,580	3,411	4,035	4,927	3,329	2,581
Official export credits[4]	222	153	236	489	341	454
Others[5]	2,358	3,258	3,798	4,438	2,988	2,127
Memorandum item						
Other official flows[6]	1,524	2,416	3,204	2,283	2,962	2,552
North Africa and Middle East	8,816	9,254	11,357	12,257	14,268	21,827
Grants[1]	3,654	3,125	3,097	3,124	5,290	5,910
ODA loans[2]	1,117	1,299	1,402	1,181	1,711	7,704
Other official credits and loans[2,3]	4,045	4,821	6,859	7,952	7,268	8,213
Official export credits[4]	379	281	342	747	1,000	1,159
Others[5]	3,665	4,541	6,517	7,205	6,268	7,055
Memorandum item						
Other official flows[6]	893	499	3,116	1,095	1,395	1,961
Asia	13,502	15,061	15,307	18,979	19,645	18,216
Grants[1]	3,715	3,975	4,558	4,901	4,999	5,516
ODA loans[2]	3,854	4,338	5,558	5,537	5,822	5,973
Other official credits and loans[2,3]	5,933	6,749	5,190	8,541	8,825	6,727
Official export credits[4]	944	828	574	784	1,326	1,546
Others[5]	4,990	5,921	4,616	7,758	7,499	5,182
Memorandum item						
Other official flows[6]	1,462	1,252	2,248	2,862	3,935	3,806
Western Hemisphere	8,852	11,278	9,116	13,009	13,572	15,053
Grants[1]	1,930	2,340	2,453	2,512	2,860	4,675
ODA loans[2]	939	957	684	1,017	999	1,669
Other official credits and loans[2,3]	5,982	7,981	5,979	9,480	9,713	8,709
Official export credits[4]	1,317	1,149	944	1,332	1,505	1,716
Others[5]	4,665	6,832	5,035	8,148	8,208	6,993
Memorandum item						
Other official flows[6]	3,333	5,040	2,784	4,104	5,681	5,121
Other[7]	2,288	2,752	3,237	3,356	2,981	2,887
Grants[1]	499	491	579	652	746	1,153
ODA loans[2]	355	479	476	357	746	732
Other official credits and loans[2,3]	1,434	1,781	2,182	2,346	1,489	1,001
Official export credits[4]	228	354	320	188	165	198
Others[5]	1,206	1,427	1,862	2,158	1,323	803
Memorandum item						
Other official flows[6]	6,270	7,396	8,431	7,885	8,506	8,582
Total (including unallocated)	50,973	60,399	63,804	74,255	78,535	85,202
Grants[1]	19,852	21,958	24,381	25,480	31,789	35,933
ODA loans[2]	7,997	9,520	10,482	10,381	12,019	18,132
Other official credits and loans[2,3]	23,124	28,921	28,941	38,394	34,728	31,137
Official export credits[4]	3,125	2,831	2,470	3,622	5,106	5,551
Others[5]	19,999	26,090	26,471	34,772	29,622	25,586
Memorandum item						
Other official flows[6]	8,315	11,799	12,719	11,238	15,581	14,855

Sources: OECD, *Geographical Distribution of Financial Flows to Developing Countries*; and data provided by the OECD.

Note: DAC denotes Development Assistance Committee of the OECD.

[1]Include debt forgiveness; estimated to have totaled $1.4 billion in 1990, and $1.9 billion in 1991.

[2]Including debt reorganization; for example, in 1991 total ODA loans to North Africa and the Middle East include a large rescheduling of Egypt's debt.

[3]Contractual lending (defined as bilateral ODA and other official loans plus officially guaranteed private export credits) less bilateral ODA loans.

[4]Direct export credits from official sources.

[5]Contractual lending (see footnote 3 above) less bilateral ODA loans and official export credits; that is, includes officially guaranteed and insured export credits and untied non-ODA official loans.

[6]Includes official export credits, untied non-ODA official loans, official sector equity and portfolio investment, and debt reorganization undertaken by the official sector on nonconcessional terms.

[7]Includes Oceania and Europe.

Table A16. Multilateral Debt by Institution, 1980–92

	1980	1985	1986	1987	1988	1989	1990	1991	1992[1]
	(In billions of U.S. dollars)								
World Bank	34.2	74.9	96.4	122.4	120.4	124.0	140.9	149.9	150.3
IBRD	22.4	50.7	68.3	89.1	84.3	84.7	95.9	100.3	97.5
IDA	11.9	24.2	28.0	33.3	36.1	39.3	45.0	49.6	52.8
Regional development banks[2]	8.3	20.1	24.4	29.5	31.8	35.5	45.3	51.2	56.5
AfDB	0.7	2.0	2.9	4.1	4.8	6.0	8.1	10.0	11.9
AsDB	2.4	5.9	6.7	7.6	8.8	10.3	15.5	18.3	20.9
IDB	5.2	12.1	14.8	17.8	18.1	19.2	21.7	22.9	23.7
European institutions[3]	2.1	4.6	6.1	8.3	8.1	9.5	11.8	13.6	14.2
Others	4.5	9.0	10.7	12.6	13.1	13.3	12.1	11.9	10.7
IMF	12.6	40.7	42.5	42.9	35.7	32.4	33.2	38.2	38.2
Total	61.8	149.2	180.1	215.7	209.1	214.8	243.3	264.9	269.9
	(In percent of total)								
World Bank	55.4	50.2	53.5	56.7	57.6	57.7	57.9	56.6	55.7
IBRD	36.2	34.0	38.0	41.3	40.3	39.4	39.4	37.9	36.1
IDA	19.2	16.2	15.6	15.4	17.3	18.3	18.5	18.7	19.6
Regional development banks[2]	13.5	13.4	13.6	13.7	15.2	16.6	18.6	19.3	20.9
AfDB	1.2	1.4	1.6	1.9	2.3	2.8	3.3	3.8	4.4
ASDB	3.9	4.0	3.7	3.5	4.2	4.8	6.4	6.9	7.8
IDB	8.4	8.1	8.2	8.3	8.7	8.9	8.9	8.6	8.8
European institutions[3]	3.4	3.1	3.4	3.9	3.9	4.4	4.9	5.2	5.3
Others	7.3	6.0	6.0	5.8	6.3	6.2	5.0	4.5	4.0
IMF	20.4	27.3	23.6	19.9	17.1	15.1	13.6	14.4	14.2
Total	100.0	100.0	100.0	100.0	100.0	100.0	100.0	100.0	100.0
Memorandum item									
Share of IDA in World Bank lending	34.8	32.3	29.0	27.2	30.0	31.7	31.9	33.1	35.1

Sources: World Bank Debtor Reporting System; and IMF staff estimates.

Note: AfDB = African Development Bank; AsDB = Asian Development Bank; IBRD = International Bank for Reconstruction and Development; IDA = International Development Association; IDB = Inter-American Development Bank.

[1]Preliminary estimate.

[2]Including development funds and other associated concessional facilities.

[3]Council of Europe, European Development Fund, European Community, and European Investment Bank.

Table A17. Net ODA Disbursements from DAC Countries, 1986–92

	1986	1987	1988	1989	1990	1991	1992[1]
				(In billions of U.S. dollars)			
Total net official development assistance (ODA)[2]	36.7	40.5	47.0	45.7	52.9	56.7	60.8
Bilateral ODA	26.2	28.8	31.9	32.9	37.1	41.3	41.3
Contributions to multilateral institutions	10.4	11.7	15.1	12.8	15.8	15.4	19.5
				(In percent)			
Share of donors' GDP							
Total ODA	0.35	0.33	0.34	0.32	0.33	0.33	0.33
Bilateral ODA	0.25	0.24	0.23	0.23	0.23	0.24	0.22
Contributions to multilateral institutions	0.10	0.09	0.11	0.09	0.10	0.09	0.11
				(In billions of U.S. dollars)			
Memorandum items							
Total ODA to developing countries[3]	39.1	43.8	47.5	48.6	52.6	57.4	58.3
DAC countries[4]	26.2	30.1	31.9	32.9	37.1	41.3	41.3
Multilateral institutions	9.3	10.0	11.0	12.3	13.4	16.1	17.0
Other[5]	3.6	3.7	4.6	3.4	2.1	—	—
By income group[6]							
Least-developed countries	10.3	11.9	13.1	13.3	15.1	14.8	15.7
Other low-income countries	10.9	11.5	14.0	14.3	17.2	19.7	21.0
Lower middle-income countries	7.3	8.5	8.2	8.2	10.4	9.4	9.8
Upper middle-income countries	3.6	3.2	3.0	3.2	4.2	4.9	4.5
Unallocated	7.0	8.7	9.2	9.6	5.7	8.6	7.3
By region[6]							
Sub-Saharan Africa[7]	10.5	12.1	14.0	14.7	17.1	17.1	17.7
North Africa and Middle East	5.0	4.8	4.6	4.6	7.3	10.8	11.6
Asia[8]	9.7	10.6	12.6	12.8	13.6	14.1	14.6
Western Hemisphere	3.7	4.3	4.3	3.9	5.3	6.0	6.2
Other[9]	10.2	12.0	12.0	12.6	9.3	9.4	8.2

Sources: OECD; and IMF staff estimates.

Note: DAC denotes Development Assistance Committee of the OECD.

[1]Provisional.

[2]Excludes debt forgiveness of non-ODA claims (including military debt) in 1990–92. Including these amounts the DAC total would be $54.3 billion in 1990, $58.5 billion in 1991, and $62.3 billion in 1992. Amounts for previous years were nil or negligible.

[3]Excludes intradeveloping country resource flows.

[4] Excludes debt forgiveness of non-ODA claims in 1990–92. Amounts in previous years were nil or negligible.

[5]Other industrial countries and unallocated.

[6]Distribution of total ODA from DAC and other sources.

[7]Includes Africa unspecified.

[8]Includes Asia unspecified.

[9]Includes Europe (outside of Central and Eastern Europe), Oceania, and unspecified.

Table A18. The World Bank: Adjustment and Project Lending Commitments, 1980–92[1]

	Project	Adjustment	Total	Adjustment Loans as Proportion of Total	Project	Adjustment	Total
	(In millions of U.S. dollars)			*(In percent)*	*(Number of loans)*		
Africa	23,542.0	11,262.2	34,804.2	32.4	946	223	1,169
1980–85	9,079.7	2,132.9	11,212.6	19.0	471	42	513
1986–90	9,946.8	6,424.4	16,371.2	39.2	339	131	470
1991–92	4,515.5	2,704.9	7,220.4	37.5	136	50	186
East Asia and Pacific	41,447.7	4,803.8	46,251.5	10.4	582	26	608
1980–85	14,164.1	1,749.8	15,913.9	10.8	272	10	282
1986–90	17,291.6	2,590.0	19,881.6	13.0	206	12	218
1991–92	9,992.0	464.0	10,456.0	4.4	104	4	108
Europe and Central Asia	17,581.8	6,585.0	22,166.7	29.7	245	29	274
1980–85	6,464.0	2,217.1	6,681.0	33.2	123	9	132
1986–90	6,150.5	2,337.9	8,488.4	27.5	80	12	92
1991–92	4,967.3	2,030.0	6,997.3	29.0	42	8	50
Latin America and Caribbean	42,623.1	16,192.3	58,815.4	29.0	545	90	635
1980–85	17,746.1	2,215.9	19,962.0	11.1	272	19	291
1986–90	17,080.2	10,741.3	27,821.5	38.6	187	45	232
1991–92	7,796.8	3,235.1	11,031.9	29.3	86	26	112
Middle East and North Africa	12,777.9	3,789.4	16,567.3	22.9	304	27	331
1980–85	6,205.9	450.4	6,656.3	6.8	165	3	168
1986–90	4,608.7	1,929.0	6,537.7	29.5	108	11	119
1991–92	1,963.3	1,410.0	3,373.3	41.8	31	13	44
South Asia	40,630.9	3,958.1	44,589.0	8.9	466	45	511
1980–85	17,183.7	763.0	17,946.7	4.3	231	13	244
1986–90	17,930.2	1,749.7	19,679.9	8.9	165	17	182
1991–92	5,517.0	1,445.4	6,962.4	20.9	70	15	85
Total	**178,603.4**	**46,590.8**	**225,194.2**	**20.7**	**3,088**	**440**	**3,528**
1980–85	70,843.5	9,529.1	80,372.6	11.9	1,534	96	1,630
1986–90	73,008.0	25,772.3	98,780.3	26.1	1,085	228	1,313
1991–92	34,751.9	11,289.4	46,041.3	24.5	469	116	585

Sources: The World Bank; and IMF staff estimates.

[1]Commitments reflect amounts approved for lending.

Table A19. Developing Country Debt to the IBRD and IDA, 1980–92

(In millions of U.S. dollars; unless otherwise indicated)

	Total Debt to IBRD and IDA				Share of IDA in Total			
	1980	1987	1990	1992	1980	1987	1990	1992
	(In billions of U.S. dollars)				*(In percent)*			
All developing countries	**34.2**	**122.4**	**140.9**	**150.4**	**34.7**	**27.2**	**31.9**	**35.1**
By region								
Sub-Saharan Africa	5.1	19.4	25.0	27.7	50.3	52.2	63.2	69.6
North Africa and the Middle East	3.1	9.2	10.0	10.7	21.9	17.4	17.4	16.8
Asia	14.1	48.3	58.8	65.3	56.6	42.5	44.3	46.0
Western Hemisphere	8.2	31.6	35.6	35.0	5.2	2.4	3.1	4.2
Other	3.7	13.9	11.2	11.7	6.5	2.2	2.8	2.8
By debt-servicing record								
Nonrescheduling countries	17.5	59.4	72.2	79.8	50.6	39.6	42.6	44.5
Rescheduling countries	16.7	63.0	68.7	70.6	18.1	15.6	20.7	24.5
Middle-income	13.2	52.1	53.8	53.4	7.3	3.3	3.2	3.4
Low-income	3.5	10.9	14.9	17.2	58.9	73.7	83.8	90.1
Memorandum item								
Selected ESAF countries[1]	2.0	6.9	9.8	11.3	75.4	86.6	92.9	95.2

Sources: World Bank Debtor Reporting System; and IMF staff estimates.

Note: IBRD denotes International Bank for Reconstruction and Development; IDA denotes International Development Association; ESAF denotes enhanced structural adjustment facility.

[1]Bangladesh, Bolivia, The Gambia, Ghana, Guyana, Lesotho, Malawi, Mozambique, Senegal, Sri Lanka, and Togo.

Table A20. Low-Income Rescheduling Countries: Debt and Debt-Service Indicators, 1980–91

(In percent; unless otherwise indicated)

	External Total Public Debt[1]			Share in Total Public Debt						Debt-Service Ratios[2]					
				Multilateral			Total concessional			Total debt[3]		Multilateral		IMF	
	1980	1987	1991	1980	1987	1991	1980	1987	1991	1987	1991	1987	1991	1987	1991
Benin	334	932	1,221	31	39	49	50	50	83	6	6	2	5	1	—
Bolivia	2,182	4,621	3,523	20	24	49	31	30	49	31	26	17	16	7	5
Burkina Faso	281	744	871	50	59	74	79	79	85	9	10	5	10	1	—
Central African Republic	146	542	802	36	47	64	40	73	86	11	6	2	4	4	2
Chad	204	267	547	37	52	71	57	74	89	3	3	2	3	1	—
Equatorial Guinea	52	173	210	5	22	33	60	51	62	22	5	2	3	4	2
Ethiopia	669	2,542	3,301	51	34	41	85	79	86	31	23	4	8	4	1
Gambia, The	97	266	321	42	60	72	70	79	84	21	12	8	4	10	3
Guinea	1,004	1,884	2,401	13	24	34	66	71	77	24	16	4	4	3	1
Guinea-Bissau	128	402	574	22	42	49	68	65	77	23	9	19	9	1	—
Guyana	598	955	1,554	18	38	34	39	48	59	9	21	3	13	1	3
Honduras	974	2,700	2,866	47	50	56	35	40	41	29	20	1	3	5	1
Liberia	515	1,117	1,127	25	38	39	42	52	52	2	—	1	—	—	—
Madagascar	892	3,150	3,381	20	28	41	54	45	63	46	28	6	8	13	8
Malawi	625	1,161	1,527	35	70	79	44	73	84	35	31	9	10	14	7
Mali	669	1,906	2,392	26	33	40	92	96	97	19	6	3	3	10	3
Mauritania	718	1,845	1,912	18	28	32	71	72	82	24	14	10	9	3	3
Mozambique	...	3,684	4,039	...	7	14	...	60	69	10	5	4	5	—	—
Nicaragua	1,661	6,349	8,703	25	14	11	28	35	35	11	121[4]	3	109[4]	—	—
Niger	383	1,244	1,278	37	38	56	41	54	65	24	8	5	3	7	4
Senegal	1,105	3,329	2,838	24	35	50	37	58	68	29	19	6	7	7	4
Sierra Leone	323	544	642	19	30	29	44	56	62	7	6	2	1	2	5
Somalia	595	1,743	1,929	27	35	39	92	80	81	33	—	5	—	27	—
Sudan	3,822	8,043	9,221	17	15	20	46	47	50	11	6	5	6	2	—
Tanzania	1,915	4,526	5,786	28	31	34	72	61	67	24	22	18	17	4	5
Togo	899	1,052	1,143	13	41	53	28	47	68	15	6	4	3	4	2
Uganda	542	1,577	2,325	16	53	62	35	55	72	38	67	8	19	23	21
Zaïre	4,261	7,205	9,151	8	17	23	21	29	35	29	8	4	4	16	3
Zambia	2,141	4,457	4,954	19	28	31	39	40	53	18	53	7	38	1	9

Sources: World Bank Debtor Reporting System; and IMF staff estimates.
[1]In millions of U.S. dollars, excluding use of IMF credit.
[2]Based on debt service actually paid. In percent of exports of goods and services.
[3]Including the IMF.
[4]Including repayment of arrears.

Table A21. Low-Income Rescheduling Countries: Disbursements from Multilateral Institutions, 1986–91

(In millions of U.S. dollars)

	Total[1]		IBRD		Other Nonconcessional		IDA		Other Concessional		IMF	
	1986–88	1989–91	1986–88	1989–91	1986–88	1989–91	1986–88	1989–91	1986–88	1989–91	1986–88	1989–91
Angola	27	54	—	—	20	30	—	—	7	25	—	—
Benin	136	254	—	—	17	17	71	145	48	72	—	21
Bolivia	881	798	5	—	358	358	157	175	135	145	226	120
Burkina Faso	178	203	—	—	34	27	74	82	70	85	—	9
Central African Republic	173	213	—	—	16	4	87	116	41	85	29	8
Chad	87	219	—	—	2	1	60	129	17	69	8	20
Equatorial Guinea	37	27	—	—	2	1	21	12	9	6	5	8
Ethiopia	354	405	—	—	13	54	200	202	100	149	41	—
Guinea	265	392	—	—	28	24	123	198	72	136	41	34
Guinea-Bissau	68	91	—	—	3	—	47	51	17	37	2	3
Guyana	59	356	1	—	35	36	6	94	17	85	—	142
Honduras	260	393	110	114	91	114	—	48	58	85	—	32
Liberia	62	—	5	—	20	—	18	—	19	—	—	—
Madagascar	573	481	—	—	55	20	268	242	144	151	106	68
Mali	302	288	—	—	7	1	150	160	116	93	29	34
Mauritania	277	198	20	—	35	5	83	65	88	107	52	22
Mozambique	201	342	—	—	26	34	116	181	18	58	41	70
Nicaragua	69	164	—	—	47	22	—	54	22	65	—	23
Niger	330	171	—	—	11	3	189	113	72	35	58	20
Senegal	767	483	13	—	32	47	295	213	238	70	189	153
Sierra Leone	59	11	—	—	—	—	12	—	24	11	23	—
Somalia	194	112	—	—	2	—	117	90	35	22	40	—
Sudan	449	465	—	—	5	23	252	282	193	160	—	—
Tanzania	516	705	15	—	21	18	311	432	43	124	126	131
Togo	193	195	—	—	15	3	119	118	20	30	39	44
Uganda	479	749	—	—	41	18	251	446	55	72	132	213
Zaïre	1,015	869	18	86	216	236	425	293	94	46	262	208
Zambia	477	438	50	—	101	93	121	217	82	128	122	—
Total countries	8,488	9,077	237	200	1,253	1,189	3,571	4,157	1,855	2,149	1,571	1,382

Sources: World Bank Debtor Reporting System; and IMF staff estimates.
Note: IBRD denotes International Bank for Reconstruction and Development; IDA denotes International Development Association.
[1]Including IMF.

Table A22. Low-Income Rescheduling Countries: Structure of Multilateral Debt, 1984–92[1]

(In millions of U.S. dollars; and percent of total)

	Stock of Multilateral Debt[2]		Shares in Total Multilateral Debt														
			Total concessional		IBRD		IDA		Regional development banks						IMF		Of which: SAF/ESAF
									Non-concessional		Concessional		Other				
	1984	1992	1984	1992	1984	1992	1984	1992	1984	1992	1984	1992	1984	1992	1984	1992	1992
Angola	18	128	14	37	—	—	—	4	1	48	—	30	99	17	—	—	—
Benin	190	661	88	94	—	—	53	59	7	1	13	19	27	21	—	—	—
Bolivia	750	2,112	45	60	23	7	12	23	40	21	—	27	15	10	8	12	11
Burkina Faso	222	679	92	89	—	—	56	54	1	4	10	15	33	27	—	—	—
Central African Republic	113	531	73	95	—	—	43	56	1	2	23	30	11	11	21	—	—
Chad	87	430	94	99	—	—	46	60	—	—	26	30	23	10	5	15	15
Equatorial Guinea	17	85	22	92	—	—	2	48	31	6	4	17	14	15	50	15	15
Ethiopia	577	1,609	81	92	8	1	66	60	3	7	7	22	4	8	13	1	1
Guinea	225	1,222	66	93	21	—	40	54	7	5	3	15	24	20	5	6	6
Guinea-Bissau	74	287	86	96	—	—	36	57	12	4	19	25	28	12	5	2	2
Guyana	299	688	48	68	18	7	8	19	28	13	—	18	21	18	24	24	15
Honduras	989	1,751	43	40	28	28	8	10	36	10	—	29	15	17	14	6	1
Liberia	436	631	23	26	19	22	14	16	9	8	1	6	9	4	48	44	—
Madagascar	531	1,554	68	93	5	1	47	57	1	4	4	18	15	12	28	7	6
Mali	409	1,093	83	97	—	—	47	56	2	2	12	21	24	15	16	6	4
Mauritania	338	655	57	91	15	5	16	35	3	2	6	14	52	35	9	9	9
Mozambique	47	872	84	88	—	—	—	48	—	8	—	15	100	9	—	20	20
Nicaragua	677	952	51	53	20	11	9	19	34	3	—	35	36	30	1	2	2
Niger	273	792	68	95	—	—	44	61	8	1	6	12	25	17	16	8	7
Senegal	692	1,796	52	89	11	3	29	49	5	3	1	9	25	20	29	15	14
Sierra Leone	173	285	49	75	5	1	27	38	4	—	6	13	15	19	43	29	6
Somalia	437	783	75	83	—	—	34	52	—	1	4	13	38	15	23	19	2
Sudan	1,481	2,474	53	65	3	—	32	46	—	1	1	9	24	10	40	34	—
Tanzania	923	2,389	73	92	22	7	56	68	3	1	4	10	12	4	3	9	9
Togo	281	703	68	94	7	—	44	66	5	2	8	8	19	13	18	11	9
Uganda	649	1,891	38	94	5	1	27	63	5	3	1	7	12	7	49	18	18
Zaïre	1,053	2,562	37	67	4	3	29	47	3	18	1	6	9	8	55	18	8
Zambia	1,185	2,453	11	43	24	12	3	26	2	8	1	5	11	14	59	34	—
Total countries	13.15	31.87	52	76	12	5	29	45	10	7	3	15	19	13	27	15	6
Total *(in millions of U.S. dollars)*	13,148	31,868	6,887	24,211	1,604	1,622	3,766	14,372	1,302	2,134	396	4,822	2,541	4,239	3,540	4,678	1,981

Sources: World Bank Debtor Reporting System; and IMF staff estimates.
Note: IBRD denotes International Bank for Reconstruction and Development; IDA denotes International Development Association; ESAF denotes enhanced structural adjustment facility; SAF denotes structural adjustment facility.
[1] 1992 figures are preliminary.
[2] Including IMF.

Table A23. Selected Low-Income Countries That Avoided Debt Reschedulings: Disbursements from Multilateral Institutions, 1986–91

(In millions of U.S. dollars)

	Total[1]		IBRD		Other Nonconcessional		IDA		Other Concessional		IMF	
	1986–88	1989–91	1986–88	1989–91	1986–88	1989–91	1986–88	1989–91	1986–88	1989–91	1986–88	1989–91
Bangladesh	2,308	2,351	—	—	60	36	987	1,036	622	961	639	318
Burundi	275	211	—	—	22	5	132	133	94	57	27	17
Gambia, The	102	83	—	—	4	2	33	32	37	29	27	19
Ghana	1,128	1,137	—	—	79	106	567	569	79	61	403	401
Kenya	692	1,209	116	21	73	118	239	639	88	143	176	288
Lesotho	74	108	—	—	9	8	22	31	39	56	4	13
Malawi	308	411	23	7	15	6	192	276	53	53	25	69
Nepal	387	482	—	—	—	—	220	229	132	244	36	10
Pakistan	1,805	4,225	663	1,179	328	960	397	453	417	723	—	910
Sri Lanka	623	1,036	14	8	1	—	225	366	171	439	213	223
Zimbabwe	199	276	81	139	58	81	22	3	38	54	—	—
Total countries	7,901	11,529	896	1,354	649	1,321	3,035	3,765	1,771	2,821	1,550	2,268

Sources: World Bank Debtor Reporting System; and IMF staff estimates.
Note: IBRD denotes International Bank for Reconstruction and Development; IDA denotes International Development Association.
[1]Includes IMF.

Table A24. Selected Low-Income Countries That Avoided Debt Reschedulings: Structure of Multilateral Debt, 1984–92[1]

(In millions of U.S. dollars; and percent of total)

	Stock of Multilateral Debt[2]		Shares in Multilateral Debt												IMF		Of which: SAF/ESAF
			Total concessional		IBRD		IDA		Regional organizations[3]		Other						
	1984	1992	1984	1992	1984	1992	1984	1992	1984	1992	1984	1992	1984	1992	1984	1992	1992
Bangladesh	2,636	8,356	86	99	2	1	64	54	14	32	7	4	14	9	9
Burundi	193	836	88	95	—	—	61	57	23	22	16	14	—	8	8
Gambia, The	98	281	62	95	—	—	31	45	19	32	23	9	27	14	14
Ghana	865	2,960	34	85	12	3	22	55	4	10	8	6	54	25	20
Kenya	1,459	3,010	33	71	40	22	25	47	2	11	7	8	26	13	11
Lesotho	103	370	93	91	—	1	52	34	30	39	19	18	—	7	7
Malawi	537	1,374	64	91	11	5	51	67	11	13	6	8	21	7	6
Nepal	370	1,595	98	100	—	—	54	48	37	44	8	5	1	3	3
Pakistan	3,730	10,016	49	56	9	24	34	25	18	38	6	3	33	11	5
Sri Lanka	881	2,768	57	97	6	2	35	40	17	35	6	7	37	17	16
Zimbabwe	423	1,204	9	30	30	37	5	11	—	19	4	15	61	18	6
Total	11,294	33,803	57	76	12	11	40	43	14	28	7	5	28	12	9
Total *(in millions of U.S. dollars)*	11,294	33,803	6,448	25,841	1,309	3,821	4,494	14,660	1,542	9,606	783	1,746	3,166	3,970	2,946

Sources: World Bank Debtor Reporting System; and IMF staff estimates.

Note: IBRD denotes International Bank for Reconstruction and Development; IDA denotes International Development Association; ESAF denotes enhanced structural adjustment facility; SAF denotes structural adjustment facility.

[1]1992 figures are preliminary.

[2] Includes IMF.

[3]Regional development banks and development funds.

Table A25. Lower Middle-Income Rescheduling Countries: Structure of Multilateral Debt, 1984–92

(In millions of U.S. dollars; and percent of total)

| | Stock of Multilateral Debt[1] | | Shares in Multilateral Debt | | | | | | | | | | | |
| | | | Total concessional | | IBRD | | IDA | | Regional development banks | | Other[2] | | IMF | |
	1984	1992	1984	1992	1984	1992	1984	1992	1984	1992	1984	1992	1984	1992
Cameroon	564	1,447	55	25	37	50	39	16	6	19	18	15	—	—
Congo	258	519	36	33	14	31	24	14	17	23	45	31	—	1
Côte d'Ivoire	1,563	3,129	7	9	49	60	—	4	2	22	10	6	38	9
Dominican Republic	666	1,000	46	43	18	26	3	2	43	59	3	2	33	12
Ecuador	891	2,374	26	22	23	33	4	1	44	56	2	6	27	4
Egypt	3,514	3,597	69	38	21	38	21	25	2	14	55	16	1	6
El Salvador	624	833	48	58	15	22	4	3	55	65	9	10	17	—
Guatemala	701	906	35	37	21	23	—	—	46	64	11	10	21	2
Jamaica	1,185	1,489	13	13	28	40	—	—	11	28	8	8	53	24
Jordan	301	1,106	54	26	28	51	28	7	—	—	44	32	—	10
Morocco	2,341	5,703	13	9	37	60	2	1	2	19	17	13	42	8
Nigeria	955	4,483	11	7	94	71	4	2	—	22	2	5	—	—
Peru	1,725	2,332	11	7	29	41	—	—	30	25	2	7	39	27
Philippines	3,596	8,064	18	21	52	52	2	2	—	—	25	32	21	14
Poland	87	1,799	—	—	—	41	—	—	—	—	100	13	—	46
Total countries			29	18	36	49	7	5	12	20	22	15	23	11
Total (in millions of U.S. dollars)	18,971	38,783	5,567	7,048	6,855	19,189	1,352	1,748	2,215	7,726	4,144	5,942	4,405	4,178
Memorandum items														
Argentina	2,660	7,427	4	1	19	34	—	—	35	35	5	—	41	31
Brazil	9,807	10,881	2	1	41	67	—	—	15	25	1	1	43	7
Bulgaria	590	1,146	—	—	—	13	—	—	—	—	100	35	—	51
Chile	1,696	5,113	6	2	13	38	1	—	40	48	—	—	46	14
Costa Rica	738	1,237	28	18	26	30	1	—	38	51	14	12	21	7
Gabon	65	438	27	6	16	19	—	—	—	—	84	63	—	18
Mexico	6,753	21,549	3	—	42	56	—	—	23	17	—	—	35	28
Panama	893	762	19	20	28	38	—	—	41	46	1	2	30	14
Romania	2,354	1,538	—	17	60	14	—	—	—	—	—	19	40	67
Trinidad and Tobago	51	551	43	3	70	6	—	—	3	33	27	10	—	51
Turkey	4,951	9,256	11	17	48	60	4	2	—	—	20	38	29	—
Yugoslavia	3,722	2,615	3	—	47	76	—	—	—	—	1	24	52	—

Sources: World Bank Debtor Reporting System; and IMF staff estimates.
Note: DAC denotes Development Assistance Committee of the OECD.
[1] Includes IMF.
[2] Includes European multilateral institutions and other.

World Economic and Financial Surveys

This series (ISSN 0258-7440) contains biannual, annual, and periodic studies covering monetary and financial issues of importance to the global economy. The core elements of the series are the *World Economic Outlook* report, usually published in May and October, and the annual report on *International Capital Markets*. Other studies assess international trade policy, private market and official financing for developing countries, exchange and payments systems, export credit policies, and issues raised in the *World Economic Outlook*.

World Economic Outlook: A Survey by the Staff of the International Monetary Fund

The *World Economic Outlook*, published twice a year in English, French, Spanish, and Arabic, presents IMF staff economists' analyses of global economic developments during the near and medium term. Chapters give an overview of the world economy; consider issues affecting industrial countries, developing countries, and economies in transition to the market; and address topics of pressing current interest. Annexes, boxes, charts, and an extensive statistical appendix augment the text.

ISSN 0256-6877.
$34.00 (academic rate: $23.00; paper).
1994 (May). ISBN 1-55775-381-4. **Stock #WEO-194.**
1994 (Oct.). ISBN 1-55775-385-7. **Stock #WEO-294.**
1993 (May). ISBN 1-55775-286-9. **Stock #WEO-193.**
1993 (Oct.). ISBN 1-55775-340-7. **Stock #WEO-293.**

International Capital Markets: Developments, Prospects, and Key Policy Issues

This annual report (in 1993, in two parts) reviews developments in international capital markets, including market integration, globalization of investor and borrower behavior, the growing imbalance between resources of private market participants and central banks, the resolution of banking crises, and the challenge posed by the growth in derivative markets.

$20.00 (academic rate: $12.00; paper).
1993. *Part I: Exchange Rate Management and International Capital Flows*, by Morris Goldstein, David Folkerts-Landau, Peter Garber, Liliana Rojas-Suarez, and Michael Spencer.
ISBN 1-55775-290-7. **Stock #WEO-693.**
1993. *Part II: Systemic Issues in International Finance*, by an IMF Staff Team led by Morris Goldstein and David Folkerts-Landau.
ISBN 1-55775-335-0. **Stock #WEO-1293.**

Staff Studies for the *World Economic Outlook*
by the IMF's Research Department

These studies, supporting analyses and scenarios of the *World Economic Outlook*, provide a detailed examination of theory and evidence on major issues currently affecting the global economy.

$20.00 (academic rate: $12.00; paper).
1993. ISBN 1-55775-337-7. **Stock #WEO-393.**
1990. ISBN 1-55775-168-4. **Stock #WEO-390.**

Developments in International Exchange and Payments Systems
by a Staff Team from the IMF's Exchange and Trade Relations Department

The global trend toward liberalization in countries' international payments and transfer systems has been most dramatic in central and Eastern Europe. But developing countries in general have brought their exchange systems more in line with market principles and moved toward more flexible exchange rate arrangements, while industrial countries have moved toward more pegged arrangements. This study reviews developments in IMF members' exchange and payments systems through March 1991.

$20.00 (academic rate: $12.00; paper).
1992. ISBN 1-55775-233-8. **Stock #WEO-892.**

Private Market Financing for Developing Countries
by a Staff Team from the IMF's Policy Development and Review Department led by Charles Collyns

This study surveys recent trends in private market financing for developing countries, including flows to developing countries through banking and securities markets; the restoration of access to voluntary market financing for some developing countries; and the status of commercial bank debt in low-income countries.

$20.00 (academic rate: $12.00; paper).
1993. ISBN 1-55775-361-X. **Stock #WEO-993.**
1992. ISBN 1-55775-318-0. **Stock #WEO-992.**

Issues and Developments in International Trade Policy
by an IMF Staff Team led by Margaret Kelly and Anne Kenny McGuirk

Since the mid-1980s, most developing countries have moved toward outward-looking, market-oriented policies and have liberalized their trade regimes. At the same time, industrial countries have acted to liberalize financial markets and foreign direct investment, deregulate services, and privatize public enterprises. This study discusses these and other developments in industrial, developing, and transition economies.

$20.00 (academic rate: $12.00; paper).
1992. ISBN 1-55775-311-3. **Stock #WEO-1092.**

Official Financing for Developing Countries
by a Staff Team from the IMF's Policy Development and Review Department led by Michael Kuhn

This study provides information on official financing for developing countries, with the focus on low- and lower-middle-income countries. It updates and replaces *Multilateral Official Debt Rescheduling: Recent Experience* and reviews developments in direct financing by official and multilateral sources.

$20.00 (academic rate: $12.00; paper)
1994. ISBN 1-55775-378-4. **Stock #WEO-1394.**

Officially Supported Export Credits: Developments and Prospects

This study examines export credit and cover policies in the ten major industrial countries.

$15.00 (academic rate: $12.00; paper).
1990. By G.G. Johnson, Matthew Fisher, and Elliot Harris.
ISBN 1-55775-139-0. **Stock #WEO-588.**
1988. By K. Burke Dillon and Luis Duran-Downing, with Miranda Xafa.
ISBN 1-55775-006-8. **Stock #WEO-587.**
